Dogs in Jumpers

15 practical knitting projects

PAVILION

Published in the United Kingdom in 2015 by
Pavilion
1 Gower Street
London
WC1E 6HD

ISBN 978-1-910496-30-5

A CIP catalogue record for this book is
available from the British Library.

10 9 8 7 6 5 4 3 2 1

Reproduction by Mission Productions Ltd,
  Hong Kong
Printed by 1010 Printing International Ltd,
  China

This book can be ordered direct from the
publisher at www.pavilionbooks.com

Photography by Kerry Jordan of
  Whippet Snippets, except portrait of
  Bruno on page 7 by Maryanne Hawes
Illustrations by Kate Haxell

All our photographs were taken on location
at the delightful Bredgar and Wormshill Light
Railway during the winter months when no
trains were running.

I would like to dedicate this book to Bruno,
my 12-year-old whippet, who is my constant
companion, my inspiration and muse.

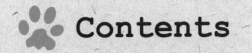

Contents

Introduction 6

Buster's Cosy Chunky Cable Jumper 8

Daisy's Really Rather Good Dog Jumper 14

Bear's Country Cable Jumper 20

Bruno's Toasty Twisted Rib Jumper 26

Pippin's Perfectly Pretty Coat 32

Textured Patchwork Blanket 38

Scout's Super-Snugly Jumper 42

Dylan's Dandy Rib Dog Jumper 48

Nelly's Properly Practical Coat 54

Frankie's Super Sloppy Joe Jumper 60

Ralph's Marvellous Multi-Coloured Jumper 66

Edie's Robust Romp-Around Jumper 70

Archie's Lovely Luxurious Jumper 76

Tinkerbell's Beautiful Basketweave Jumper 82

Gladys's Roomy Raglan Jumper 88

Abbreviations 94

Measure Your Dog 95

Top Tips 96

Introduction

It all started some 12 years ago when I decided it was time to have a whippet in my life! I had always loved the breed; we had a rescue whippet when I was growing up. When I met my vet's beautiful whippet puppy, Frodo, I knew the time was right. It was clearly meant to be, because Frodo's parents were due to have another litter. Three months later

I picked up Bruno, having fallen utterly in love with him when he was just four days old, even though he looked more like a guinea pig than a whippet!

Some months after Bruno's arrival, it transpired that my little bundle of love on long legs suffered from alopecia, and so really felt the cold. Easy to solve that, I thought; I will take to the Internet and order him a jumper. Not so easy. Jumpers were on offer – plenty of them – but getting good quality and a good fit seemed impossible. Bruno and I bumbled through our first winter, but I would have to do something to keep him warm by the next.

I was taught to knit, and sew, by my mother, but by the age of 13 I had lost interest in knitting in favour of hair, makeup and going to the school disco, so the needles and yarn were packed away. Some 30 years later, with a shivering whippet beside me, I decided it was time to get the needles and the yarn out again. This is when my love of knitting took over my life! It truly became an addiction for me. Bruno got a jumper that winter, but it was clear that I needed to polish up my skills if he was ever going to have a garment that we could both be proud of.

Over the next couple of years I booked myself into knitting workshops and improved my rather basic skills to the level where I could tackle intricate lace knitting. I learned how to knit Fair Isle and cable designs, two styles that remain favourites to this day. I also learned how to finish my garments professionally, and how to knit in the round.

At that time I had a gift shop and Bruno, in the many jumpers I made him, became the envy of all shivering, short-haired dogs who visited. The orders started to come in, and soon I added some machine-knitted jumpers and other dog products to the range. Then the shop was sold and my company, Redhound for Dogs, was born.

Since then I have developed a range of dog jumpers that sell as kits, and now I'm thrilled to have the opportunity to design more jumpers especially for this book. There are styles to suit dogs of many shapes and sizes, all made with both practicality and good looks in mind.

So measure your dog (turn to page 95 to see how), choose a project and show your own dog how much you love them!

Debbie Humphreys

PAW-ABILITY LEVEL

Each project has a paw-rated ability level, with one paw for a pattern that is quite straightforward, up to three paws for more challenging knits.

🐾 FACT FILE

BUSTER

Breed: Greyhound.
Character: Very loving and happy boy, especially when he is with his humans. He loves a family get-together as it gives plenty of counter-surfing opportunities!
Happiest When: Walking on Camber Sands.
Will Do Anything For: Treats – any kind!
Naughtiest Habit: Raiding the waste bin.
Favourite Treat: Fish and potato biscuits.
Hobbies Include: Sleeping on the sofa with his teddy bear.

Buster's Cosy Chunky Cable Jumper

I designed this jumper knowing that the green and the chunky cable would look fantastic on Buster. Mark off the pattern rows as you complete them. Knitting in the round makes the cable easier as you are looking at the right side of the work, so the pattern is a pleasure to knit.

Size
Dog measurements
Neck 43cm
Shoulder 33cm
Chest 71–75cm
Length 70–75cm
See Measure Your Dog
   (page 95)

Garment measurements
Neck 40cm unstretched
Chest 61cm unstretched
Length 58cm plus collar

Yarn
8 x 50g balls of Rowan Felted
   Tweed Aran in Glade 733

Needles and equipment
One each of 4.5mm and 5mm
   circular needles
Set of 5 x 4mm double-pointed
   needles
Cable needle
4 stitch markers
3 stitch holders
Knitter's sewing needle

Tension
27sts and 26 rows over central
   cable patt to a 10cm square
   using 5mm needles.

Abbreviations
See page 94.

Notes
This jumper is knitted for the most part in the round on a circular needle, and the pattern assumes that the rs is the inside of the knitting.

JUMPER
Starting at the neck edge and with 4.5mm circular needle, cast on 105sts. Ensuring that the work is not twisted, place marker and join the round.
Round 1: [k3, p2] to end.
This round sets rib patt. Cont in patt until rib measures 23cm from cast on edge.
The inside of the tube of knitting is k3, p2 rib and will be the rs of the neck rib when the neck is rolled down, so now turn the work inside out and work the neck inc.
Next round (inc round): [p3, k1, M1, k1] to end. *(126sts)*
Next round: [p3, k3] to end.

The last row sets new rib patt. Cont in patt until rib measures 26cm from cast on edge. Change to 5mm circular needle. Divide sts to form back sts, first leg sts, chest sts and second leg sts as folls:

Round 1: k6, p3, [k9, p3] 5 times, k6 (*75sts for back*), place marker, [k3, p3] twice, k3 (*15sts for first leg*), place marker, [p3, k3] 3 times, p3 (*21sts for chest*), place marker, [k3, p3] twice, k3 (*15sts for second leg*).

Round 2 (inc round): k1, M1, k5, p3, [k9, p3] 5 times, k5, M1, k1 across back sts (*77sts for back*), slm, rib as set across leg and chest sts, slm.

Round 3 (cable round): k7, p3, [k3, C6F, p3] 5 times, k7 across back sts, slm, rib as set across leg and chest sts, slm.

Round 4: k7, p3, [k9, p3] 5 times, k7 across back sts, slm, rib as set across leg and chest sts, slm.

Round 5: k7, p3, [k9, p3] 5 times, k7 across back sts, slm, rib as set across leg and chest sts, slm.

Round 6 (inc round): k1, M1, k6, p3, [k9, p3] 5 times, k6, M1, k1 across back sts (*79sts for back*), slm, rib as set across leg and chest sts, slm.

Round 7 (cable round): k8, p3, [C6B, k3, p3] 5 times, k8 across back sts, slm, rib as set across leg and chest sts, slm.

Round 8: k8, p3, [k9, p3] 5 times, k8 across back sts, slm, rib as set across leg and chest sts, slm.

These 8 rounds set patt. Cont in patt, inc on every round 2 and 6 until there are 89sts on back sts and 140sts in total. (*89sts for back, 15sts for first leg, 21sts for chest, 15sts for second leg*) Cont without shaping until work measures 35cm from cast on edge. At this stage you can adjust length to suit your dog.

Make leg holes

Next round: work back sts in patt, rib across 15 first leg sts then put them onto a stitch holder, rib across 21 chest sts, rib across 15 second leg sts then put them onto a stitch holder.

Next round: work back sts in patt, cast on 15sts for first leg, rib across 21 chest sts, cast on 15sts for second leg, ensuring the markers are in place again. Cont in the round in patt as set until work measures 20cm from leg holes.

Shape under chest

Next round (dec round): work back sts in patt, rib across first leg sts to 2sts before marker, k2tog *(14sts for first leg)*, slm,

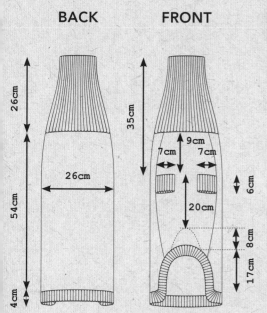

BACK   FRONT

rib across 21 chest sts, slm, k2tog, rib across rem leg sts *(14sts for second leg)*.
Cont to dec as set, altering the dec worked (either k2tog or p2tog) to suit patt, until all 15sts of each leg are eliminated. On the last dec round, remove the markers.
Cont without decreasing until work measures 28cm from leg holes, finishing with patt round 7.
Next round: work back sts in patt as set for round 8, rib across 21 chest sts then put them onto a stitch holder.
Work back sts, working back and forth on the circular needle.
Row 1 (rs): k13, p3, [k9, p3] 5 times, k13.
Row 2: p13, k3, [p9, k3] 5 times, p13.
Row 3 (cable row): k13, p3, [k3, C6F, p3] 5 times, k13.
Row 4: p13, k3, [p9, k3] 5 times, p13.
Row 5: k13, p3, [k9, p3] 5 times, k13.
Row 6: p13, k3, [p9, k3] 5 times, p13.
Row 7 (cable row): k13, p3, [C6B, k3, p3] 5 times, k13.

Row 8: p13, k3, [p9, k3] 5 times, p13.
These 8 rows set cable patt with st st borders.

Shape rump
Dec on every row 1 and row 5 of cable patt rep by working k2tog, 3sts in from each edge, then working rem sts of st st border until 71sts remain and work measures 54cm from bottom of neck rib along centre back of jumper.

Rib border
With 4.5mm circular needle, k2, k2tog, [p3, k3] 10 times, p3, k2tog, k2, pick up 27sts along the right side back panel edge, [k3, p3] 3 times, k3 across chest sts on stitch holder, pick up 27sts along the left side back panel edge to complete the round.
Place marker and commence working in the round.
Next round: [k3, p3] to end.
Rep this round until rib measures 4cm, then cast off loosely in patt. It is important that you don't cast off too tightly, as this edge needs to stretch over the dog's chest when pulling the jumper on and off.

LEG HOLE BORDER
Working with the jumper rs out and using 4mm dpns, on one leg hole pick up 21sts across cast off leg hole sts, then rib the 15sts from the holder. Divide the sts between 4 dpns (9sts on each needle).
Round 1: k3, place marker, [p3, k3] to end.
Work in rib as set for 14 rounds. Cast off loosely in patt.
Work second leg hole border to match.

TO MAKE UP
Weave in all loose ends.

🐾 FACT FILE

MISS
·········
DAISY DUKE
·····················

Breed: Miniature Smooth-Haired Dachshund.

Character: Daisy has a big character! She knows what she wants and she knows how to get it!

Happiest When: Her tummy is full and she can settle with her human dad for a cuddle.

Will Do Anything For: Food, treats and her bed.

Naughtiest Habit: Pulling her brother's tail to get his attention for playtime.

Favourite Treat: Sprats.

Hobbies Include: Barking, running, eating, sleeping and chasing pheasants.

Daisy's Really Rather Good Dog Jumper

I wanted textured stripes to flatter a dachshund's long body and this easy twist stitch is great in what is effectively a rib pattern. There is shaping to accommodate the deep chest of these little dogs and short legs so that the jumper does not slip off when the dog runs around.

Size

Dog measurements
Neck 24–30cm
Shoulder 12–14cm
Chest 38–44cm
Length 35–39cm
See Measure Your Dog
(page 95)

Garment measurements
Neck 26cm unstretched
Chest 40cm unstretched
Length 35cm plus collar

Yarn

3 x 50g balls of Rowan Felted
Tweed Aran in Dark Violet 738

Needles and equipment

Pair each of 4mm and 4.5mm
knitting needles
4 safety pins to use as markers
for leg holes
Knitter's sewing needle

Tension

22sts and 24 rows over twist rib
patt to a 10cm square using
4.5mm needles.

Abbreviations

See page 94.

TOP PANEL

Starting at the lower edge and with 4mm needles, cast on 50sts.
Set rib patt
Row 1 (rs): k4, [p2, k2] to last 6sts, p2, k4.
Row 2: k2, [p2, k2] to end.
Rep last 2 rows 4 times more.
Row 11 (dec row): k2, k2tog, [p2, k2] to last 6sts, p2, k4. *(49sts)*
Row 12: knit the knit sts and purl the purl sts.
Change to 4.5mm needles.
Set twist rib patt
Row 1 (rs): p1, [Tw2, p3] to last 3sts, Tw2, p1.
Row 2: k1, [p2, k3] to last 3sts, p2, k1.
These 2 rows set twist rib patt.
Cont in patt until work measures 23cm from cast on edge, ending with a ws row.
Shape leg
Next row (rs): cast off 4sts, patt to end. *(45sts)*

Next row: cast off 4sts, patt to end. *(41sts)*
Cont in rib patt as set until work measures 7cm from start of leg shaping.
Place a marker at each edge of work to mark end of leg hole.
Cont in rib patt as set until work measures 12cm from start of leg shaping, dec 1st in centre of last row.
With rs facing put these 40sts onto a stitch holder and set aside.

UNDER PANEL

Starting at the lower edge and with 4.5mm needles, cast on 18sts.
Set rib patt
Row 1 (rs): k3, [p2, k3] twice, p2, k3.
Row 2: k1, p2, [k2, p3] twice, k2, p2, k1.
Rep last 2 rows twice more.
Row 7 (inc row): k2, M1, k1, [p2, k3] twice, p2, k1, M1, k2. *(20sts)*
Row 8: k1, p3, [k2, p3] twice, k2, p3, k1.
Keeping edge sts as st st, cont to inc and work into st st on every 4th row as set until there are 38sts. Knit the first and last stitch on ws rows to give a neat edge.
Cont without shaping until work measures 18cm from cast on edge, ending with a ws row.
Shape leg
Next row (rs): cast off 4sts, k8, [p2, k3] twice, p2, k13. *(34sts)*
Next row: cast off 4sts, p8, [k2, p3] twice, k2, p8, k1. *(30sts)*
Next row (dec row): k2, k2tog, k5, [p2, k3] twice, p2, k5, k2tog, k2. *(28sts)*
Next row: k1, p7, [k2, p3] twice, k2, p7, k1.
Keeping edge sts as st st, dec

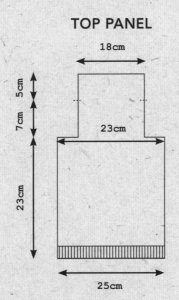

TOP PANEL

18cm
5cm
7cm
23cm
23cm
25cm

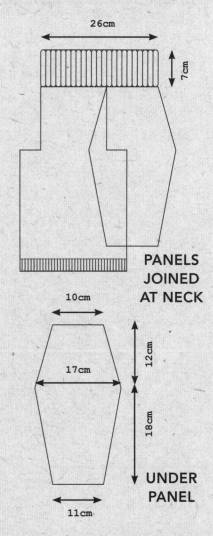

26cm
7cm

PANELS JOINED AT NECK

10cm
17cm
12cm
18cm
11cm

UNDER PANEL

by working 2sts together in this way on next and every 4th row until there are 18sts. Cont without shaping until leg hole measures 7cm. Place a marker at each edge

to mark where leg hole ends.
Cont straight in patt until work
matches top panel from leg hole,
ending with a ws row.

Joining the neck
Change to 4mm needles.
Next row (rs): [k2, p2] 4 times,
k2, then with rs facing, [p2, k2]
across the 40sts of the top panel
on the holder.
Work as set until rib measures
7cm, then cast off loosely in patt.

TO MAKE UP
Join the shoulder seams down
to marker, reversing seam on last
4cm of neck to fold over.

Leg hole border
With 4mm needles and rs facing,
pick up 30sts along the leg hole.
It doesn't matter if you pick up
more stitches, but do not pick
up fewer, and ensure you have
a number divisible by 4 plus 2.

Set rib patt
Next row (ws): [k2, p2] to last
2sts, k2.
Next row: [p2, k2] to last 2sts, p2.
Rep last 2 rows once more, then
the first row once again.
Cast off loosely in patt.
Repeat for the second leg.

Sew up the leg seams and then
sew the top panel to the under
panel, noting that the under
panel is shorter.
Weave in all loose ends.

🐾 FACT FILE

BEAR
....

Breed: Welsh Terrier.
Character: A true terrier, intensely focused one minute, easily distracted the next. Intelligent, alert, fun and very loyal.
Happiest When: Chasing rabbits in the spring sunshine; travelling to exciting places with his devoted owner, Verity.
Will Do Anything For: Peanut butter or Quavers.
Favourite Treat: Ice cream.
Hobbies Include: Travelling, digging up molehills and going to the pub.

Bear's Country Cable Jumper

I am fascinated by cables and the effects you can achieve with them and I love how the twists give a straightforward rib design a marvellous texture. The single rib adds a vintage feel that suits this handsome chap very well. This yarn is machine-washable, so your dog can get as grubby as he likes!

Size

Dog measurements
Neck 26–34cm
Shoulder 16–20cm
Chest 50–60cm
Length 44–47cm
See Measure Your Dog
(page 95)

Garment measurements
Neck 24cm unstretched
Chest 46cm unstretched
Length 44cm plus collar

Yarn

2 x 100g balls of Rowan Pure Wool Worsted in Hazel 128

Needles and equipment

Pair of 4mm knitting needles
Cable needle
4 safety pins to use as markers for leg holes
Knitter's sewing needle

Tension

32sts and 29 rows over cable patt (slightly stretched) to a 10cm square using 4mm needles.

Abbreviations

See page 94.

TOP PANEL

Starting at the lower edge and with 4mm needles, cast on 61sts.

Set rib patt
Row 1 (rs): k2, [p1, k1] to last 3sts, p1, k2.
Row 2: k1, [p1, k1] to last 2sts, p1, k1.
Rep last 2 rows 4 times more.

Set cable patt
Row 1 (inc row) (rs): k5, [p3, k4] 7 times, p3, k3, M1, k1. *(62sts)*
Row 2: k1, [p4, k3] to last 5sts, p4, k1.
Row 3: k1, [C2F, C2B, p3] to last 5sts, C2F, C2B, k1.
Row 4: k1, [p4, k3] to last 5sts, p4, k1.
Row 5 (inc row): k1, M1, k4, [p3, k4] 7 times, p3, k4, M1, k1. *(64sts)*
Row 6: k1, p5, k3, [p4, k3] to last 6sts, p5, k1.
Row 7: k1, p1, [C2F, C2B, p3] to last 6sts, C2F, C2B, p1, k1.
Row 8: k2, [p4, k3] to last 6sts, p4, k2.
Rows 5–8 set cable patt with incs on every row 5. Work as set until there are 86sts, working the incs into the p3, k4 rib patt, and into the cable patt as enough stitches become available.
Then work straight (without incs) in patt until work measures approximately 25cm from cast on

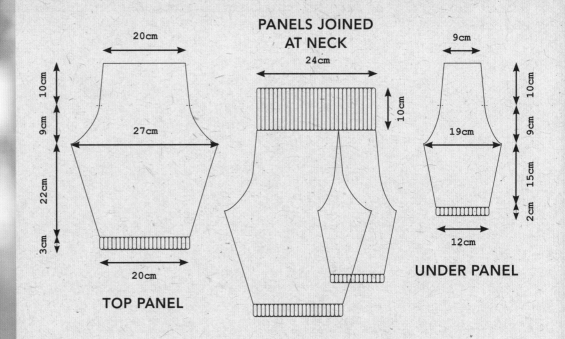

PANELS JOINED AT NECK

20cm · 10cm · 9cm · 27cm · 22cm · 3cm · 20cm

TOP PANEL

24cm · 10cm

9cm · 10cm · 9cm · 19cm · 15cm · 2cm · 12cm

UNDER PANEL

edge, ending with row 8 (last row) of patt rep.

Shape leg

Keeping cable patt as set:

Next row (rs): cast off 3sts, p3, [k4, p3] to last 3sts, k3. *(83sts)*

Next row: cast off 3sts, k3, [p4, k3] to end. *(80sts)*

Next row (dec row): k1, p2tog, patt to last 3sts, p2tog, k1. *(78sts)*

Next row: k2, p4, [k3, p4] to last 2sts, k2.

Keeping cable and rib patt as set, dec by working 2sts together in patt, 1st in from each edge, on the next row and every 4th row (row 5) of patt rep.

Cont to dec as set until there are 68sts. Cont without shaping until work measures approximately 34cm from cast on edge, ending with row 8 (last row) of patt rep.

Place a marker 9cm from start of leg shaping to mark top of leg hole.

Shape shoulder

Next row (rs): k1, k2tog, patt to last 3sts, k2tog, k1. *(66sts)*

Keeping cable and rib patt as set,

dec on every 4th row until there are 52sts. The work should now measure approximately 44cm from cast on edge.

Work 4 more rows of patt, dec by working 2sts together in patt, 1st in from each edge, on every row, work 1 row, then put these 44sts onto a stitch holder and set aside.

UNDER PANEL

Starting at the lower edge and with 4mm needles, cast on 36sts.

Set rib patt

Row 1 (rs): k3, [p2, k2] to last 5sts, p2, k3.

Row 2: k1, p2, [k2, p2] to last 5sts, k2, p2, k1.

These 2 rows set rib patt.

Cont in patt until rib measures 2cm from cast on edge, ending with a ws row.

Next row (inc row) (rs): k2, M1, k1, [p2, k2] to last 5sts, p2, k1, M1, k2. *(38sts)*

Next row: k1, p3, [k2, p2] to last 6sts, k2, p3, k1.

Keeping edge sts as st st, cont to inc on every 4th row as set until there are 48sts. Knit the first and last stitch on ws rows to give a neat edge.

Cont without shaping as set until work measures 17cm from cast on edge, ending with a ws row.

Leg shaping

Next row (rs): cast off 6sts, patt to end. *(42sts)*

Next row: cast off 6sts, patt to end. *(36sts)*

Next row (dec row): k2, k2tog, patt to last 4sts, k2tog, k2. *(34sts)*

Next row: k1, patt to last st, k1.

Keeping patt as set, dec on next and every 4th row until there are 26sts.

Cont straight, place a marker 9cm from start of leg shaping to mark top of leg hole, then cont straight until work matches top panel from leg hole, ending with a ws row.

Join the neck

With rs facing on under panel, set neck rib by working [k1, p1] across these 26sts, then with rs facing cont in rib across the 44sts of the top panel on the holder. Work in patt until rib measures 10cm, cast off loosely in patt.

TO MAKE UP

Block the top panel, and the sides of the under panel. Sew up the shoulder seam from the bottom of the neck rib down to the markers at the top of the leg hole. For the other shoulder seam, turn the work inside out, and starting at the neck edge and using mattress stitch, sew 5cm of the seam, then turn work back to right side and finish the seam down to the markers at the top of the leg hole.

Leg hole border

With rs facing, pick up 41sts along the leg hole, from the leg shaping on the top panel, up to the shoulder seam and down to the start of the leg shaping on the under panel. It doesn't matter if you pick up more stitches, but do not pick up fewer, and ensure you have an odd number.

Set rib patt

Next row (ws): p1, [k1, p1] to end.

Next row: k1, [p1, k1] to end.

Rep last 2 rows 3 times more.

Cast off loosely in patt on ws.

Work second leg to match.

Sew up leg seams and then sew the top panel to the under panel.

🐾 FACT FILE

BRUNO
....

Breed: Whippet.
Character: A devoted companion, fond of treats, warm jumpers and comfy beds.
Happiest When: He has stolen any item of human food.
Will Do Anything For: Cheese.
Naughtiest Habit: Unlike Scout, the list is endless.
Favourite Treat: Dried fish skin, jerky, dried venison; the list goes on and on…
Hobbies Include: Chasing and catching his Frisbee or ball, sleeping under the sofa throw and barking at the treat cupboard door.

Bruno's Toasty Twisted Rib Jumper

This stitch pattern creates a mini-cable effect that isn't difficult to work; just mark off the rows as you complete them and once the pattern is established it is easy to follow. I have used a contrast colour for the under panel, neck and leg rib but you can use one colour throughout.

Size
Dog measurements
Neck 26–32cm
Shoulder 19–22cm
Chest 60–72cm
Length 61–65cm
See Measure Your Dog
   (page 95)

Garment measurements
Neck 32cm unstretched
Chest 62cm unstretched
Length 55cm plus collar

Yarn
4 x 50g balls of Rowan Felted
   Tweed Aran in Flint (mc) and
   2 x 50g balls in Pebble (cc)

Needles and equipment
Pair each of 4mm and 5mm
   knitting needles
4 safety pins to use as markers
   for leg holes
1 stitch holder
Knitter's sewing needle

Tension
22sts and 26 rows over twisted
   rib patt to a 10cm square using
   5mm needles.

Abbreviations
See page 94.

TOP PANEL
Starting at the lower edge with cc and 4mm needles, cast on 66sts.
Row 1 (rs): k4, [p2, k2] to last 6sts, p2, k4.
Row 2: k2, [p2, k2] to end.
These 2 rows set rib patt.
Change to mc.
Rep last 2 rows 4 times more.
Change to 5mm needles.
Set twisted rib patt
Row 1 (rs): knit.
Row 2: k2, [p2, k2] to end.
Row 3: p2, [T.2, p2] to end.
Row 4: k1, p to last st, k1.
These 4 rows set rib patt. Work these 4 rows once more.
Shape rump
Next row (inc row) (rs): k1, M1, k to last 2sts, M1, k1. (*68sts*)
Next row: k3, [p2, k2] to last 5sts, p2, k3.
Next row: k1, p2, [T.2, p2] to last 5sts, T.2, p2, k1.
Next row: k1, p to last st, k1.

Keeping twisted rib patt correct, inc as set on every alt row 1 (that is, every 8 rows) until there are 78sts, ending with patt row 4. Set new patt.

Row 1 (rs): knit.

Row 2: p2, [k2, p2] to end.

Row 3: k2, p2, [T.2, p2] to last 2sts, k2.

Row 4: k1, p to last st, k1.

Cont in patt as set until panel measures 33cm from cast on edge, finishing with patt row 4.

Shape leg

Next row (rs): cast off 4sts, k to end. *(74sts)*

Next row: cast off 4sts, p1, [k2, p2] to end. *(70sts)*

Work rows 3–4 of patt, keeping patt as set.

Next row (dec row): k2, k2tog, k to last 4sts, k2tog, k2. *(68sts)*

Next row: p1, [k2, p2] to last 3sts, k2, p1.

Next row: k1, p2, [T.2, p2] to last st, k1.

Next row: k1, p to last st, k1.

Dec as above on next and foll row 1 of patt rep. *(64sts)*

Cont in patt without shaping until leg hole measures 10cm, ending with patt row 4.

Place a marker at each end of row to mark bottom of leg hole.

Shape shoulder

Next row (dec row) (rs): k2, k2tog, knit to last 4sts, k2tog, k2. *(62sts)*

Work rows 2–4 of patt, keeping patt as set.

Dec as set on every patt row 1, keeping patt correct, until there are 50sts, and then work straight until panel measures 55cm from cast on edge.

Place these 50sts onto a stitch holder.

UNDER PANEL

Starting at the lower edge and with 4mm needles and cc, cast on 40sts.

Next row (rs): k3, [p2, k2] to last 5sts, p2, k3.

Next row: k1, p2, [k2, p2] to last 5sts, k2, p2, k1.

These 2 rows set rib patt.

Cont in patt until rib measures

TOP PANEL

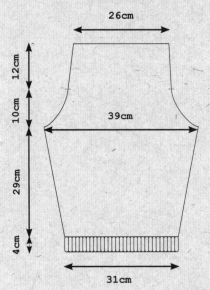

PANELS JOINED AT NECK

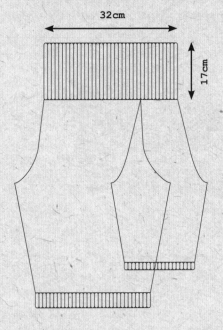

2cm from cast on edge, ending with a ws row.

Set twisted rib patt

Next row (inc row) (rs): k2, M1, p2, [T.2, p2] to last 3sts, M1, k2. *(42sts)*

Next row: k1, p3, [k2, p2] to last 6sts, k2, p3, k1.

Next row: k4, p2, [k2, p2] to last 4sts, k4.

Next row: k1, p3, [k2, p2] to last 6sts, k2, p3, k1.

Next row (inc row) (rs): k2, M1, k1, p2, [T.2, p2] to last 4sts, k1, M1, k2. *(44sts)*

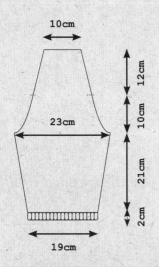

UNDER PANEL

These 4 rows set central twisted rib patt with st st borders. Knit the first st on every ws row to give a neat edge.

Keeping patt correct, inc and work into st st as set 2sts in from edge on every foll 8th row until there are 54sts.

Cont to work as set until panel measures 23cm from cast on edge, ending with a ws row.

Shape leg

Next row (rs): cast off 4sts, patt to end. *(50sts)*

Next row: cast off 4sts, patt to end. *(46sts)*

Next row (dec row): k2, k2tog, patt to last 4sts, k2tog, k2. *(44sts)*

Next row: work as patt.

Next row: dec, working k2tog as set. *(42sts)*

Cont in patt with no shaping until leg hole measures 10cm.

Place a marker at each end of row to mark top of leg hole.

Shape shoulder

Dec, working k2tog as above, on next and every alt row until there are 26sts.

Cont in patt with no shaping until under panel matches top panel from leg to shoulder seam, ending a ws row.

Join neck

With 4mm needles and mc, [p2, k2] across the 26 under panel sts, [p2, k2] the 50 top panel sts to last 2sts, k2. *(76sts)*

Cont in rib patt until neck rib measures 15cm.

Change to cc.

Cont in rib for a further 2cm.

Cast off loosely in patt.

TO MAKE UP

Join the shoulder seams down to the marker, turning the seam to the other side halfway down the neck rib so that the seam does not show when the neck is rolled down on the right side.

Leg hole border

With rs facing, 4mm needles and mc, pick up 42sts along the leg hole, from the leg shaping on the top panel, up to the shoulder seam and down to the beginning of the leg shaping on the under panel. It doesn't matter if you pick up more stitches, but do not pick up fewer, and ensure you have a number divisible by 4 plus 2.

Set rib patt

Next row (ws): [p2, k2] to last 2sts, p2.

Next row: [k2, p2] to last 2sts, k2.

Rep last 2 rows 8 times more.

Change to cc.

Work 2 more rows in rib.

Cast off loosely in patt.

Repeat for the second leg.

Sew up the side seams from the legs down; the under panel is 10cm shorter than the top panel.

Weave in all loose ends.

 # FACT FILE

PIPPIN,
AKA PIPSQUEAK

Breed: Miniature Schnauzer.
Character: Busy, alert and happy. Loves to police the front garden from the sofa when left alone – a prohibited activity when family are home!
Happiest When: Off the lead on a walk. Also snorting and leaping around after a bath.
Will Do Anything For: Roast meat.
Naughtiest Habit: Waiting under the chopping board for a morsel to fall her way.
Favourite Treat: Peanut butter- and marmite-stuffed Kong toy.
Hobbies Include: Chasing squirrels and pigeons.

Pippin's Perfectly Pretty Coat

I discovered this stitch in a vintage pattern and I love it, especially done in this retro shade of pink. It is an easy stitch to work but requires concentration because it is tricky to unravel to make a correction. So mark off your rows and don't let anyone talk to you until a row is ticked off!

Size
Dog measurements
Neck 26–34cm
Shoulder 16–20cm
Chest 54–66cm
Length 41cm
See Measure Your Dog
  (page 95)

Garment measurements
Neck 24cm unstretched
Chest 45cm unstretched
Length 38cm plus collar

Yarn
2 x 100g balls of Rowan Pure
  Wool Worsted in Satin 116
(Note that this size takes all of 200g, so if you are adding any length you will need a third ball.)

Needles and equipment
Pair each of 4mm and 4.5mm
  knitting needles
4 stitch holders
Knitter's sewing needle
2 buttons

Tension
18sts and 22 rows over stitch
  patt to a 10cm square using
  4.5mm needles.

Abbreviations
See page 94.

MAIN PATTERN
Row 1 (rs): k2, [k1b, k1] to last st, k1.
Row 2: knit.
Row 3: [k1, k1b] to last st, k1.
Row 4: knit.
These 4 rows form patt rep.

TOP PANEL
Starting at the lower edge and with 4mm needles, cast on 90sts.
Row 1 (rs): k4, [p2, k2] to last 6sts, p2, k4.
Row 2: k2, [p2, k2] to end.
These 2 rows set rib patt. Cont in patt until rib measures 5cm from cast on edge, ending with row 1.
Next row (dec row): k2, [p2, k2] to last 12sts, p2tog, k2, p2, k2, p2, k2. *(89sts)*
Cut yarn.
Change to 4.5mm needles.
Next row: place 10sts onto a stitch holder, rejoin yarn, work main patt across next 69sts, place 10sts onto a stitch holder.

Work in patt across 69sts until work measures 38cm from cast on edge, ending with a ws row.

Divide for neck

Next row (rs): Patt across 19sts, place next 31sts on one stitch holder and the next 19sts on another stitch holder.

*__Next row:__ work in patt on these 19sts until panel measures 13cm from division of neck.

Cast off.*

Rejoin yarn to rem 19sts on stitch holder and rep from * to *.

Neck rib

With right side facing, pick up 26sts along right side of neck, knit across 31sts on stitch holder, pick up 25sts along left side of neck. *(82sts)*

Next row (ws): p2, [k2, p2] to end.

Next row: k2, [p2, k2] to end.

These 2 rows set rib patt. Cont in patt until rib measures 10cm.

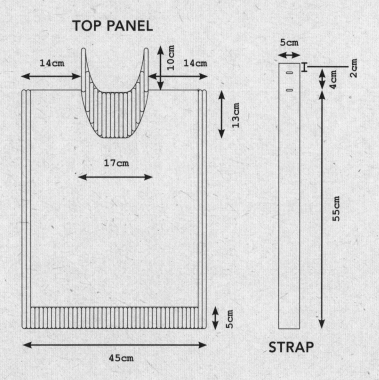

TOP PANEL

14cm · 10cm · 14cm · 13cm · 17cm · 5cm · 45cm

5cm · 2cm · 4cm · 55cm

STRAP

Cast off loosely in patt.

Rib border

Put 10 edge sts on stitch holder on right side of coat onto 4mm needles and rejoin yarn.

*Next row (rs): k4, p2, k2, p2.

Next row: k2, p2, k2, p2, k2.

These 2 rows set rib patt. Cont in patt until, without stretching it, rib measures the same as the main panel. (You may find it easiest to sew the rib on as you work it to get the length right.) Cast off.*

Rejoin yarn to rem 10sts on stitch holder and rep from * to *.

STRAP

Using 4mm needles, cast on 10sts.

Row 1 (rs): k4, p2, k4.

Row 2: k2, p2, k2, p2, k2.

These 2 rows set strap rib patt. Cont in patt until strap measures 55cm from cast on edge, ending with a ws row. At this stage you can adjust strap length to suit your dog.

Next row: k4, yo, p2tog, k4.

Cont in patt until strap measures 59cm from cast on edge, ending with a ws row.

Next row: k4, yo, p2tog, k4.
Cont in patt until strap measures 61cm from cast on edge.
Cast off.

TO MAKE UP
Block main body panel and rib borders. Sew both rib borders to the top panel. Sew up the centre front seam. When you reach halfway up the neck, turn the seam to sew from the wrong side so that the seam does not show when the neck rib is rolled down. Position the strap across the middle of the top panel, with 11cm of the buttonhole side to the left of the coat, and sew on the strap securely through all layers at the centre top of the coat. Sew on buttons (I used two vintage ones) to other end of strap to align with buttonholes. Weave in all loose ends.

Textured Patchwork Blanket

Whippets especially love to burrow into cosy blankets. If you knit a square in an evening, you will soon have enough to sew together. Three of the stitch patterns are also featured in jumpers in this book, so the squares make excellent practice if you are not a confident knitter.

Size
Finished blanket measures approximately 80 x 80cm

Yarn
2 x 100g balls of Rowan Pure Wool Worsted in each of Oats 152, Light Navy 153, Apple 129 and Bottle 140

Needles and equipment
Pair of 5mm knitting needles
Cable needle
Knitter's sewing needle

Tension
All tensions over patt to a 10cm square using 5mm needles.
Pattern 1: 17sts and 20 rows.
Pattern 2: 22sts and 30 rows.
Pattern 3: 21sts and 31 rows.
Pattern 4: 22sts and 32 rows.

Note that this blanket consists of four 20cm squares each of four different patterns; they all knit up slightly differently, so do check the measurements of each carefully to make sure that they are all the same size.

Abbreviations
See page 94.

PATTERN 1:
KNIT BELOW STITCH
Make 4 in Oats.
Note that Pattern 1 is very stretchy and you might have to cast on fewer sts to achieve 20cm, or go down a size to 4mm needles.
Mark the rows off as you knit as this pattern is hard to count, and very hard to unravel.
Cast on 35sts.
Knit one row.
Row 1 (rs): k2, [k1b, k1] to last st, k1.
Row 2: knit.
Row 3: [k1, k1b] to last st, k1.
Row 4: knit.
Rep rows 1–4 until work measures 20cm from cast on edge.
Cast off.

PATTERN 2:
FLAT CABLE
Make 4 in Light Navy.
Cast on 44sts.
Row 1 (rs): [p4, k4] to last 4sts, p4.
Row 2: [k4, p4] to last 4sts, k4.

Row 3: knit.
Row 4: purl.
Row 5: [k4, C4F] to last 4sts, k4.
Row 6: purl.
Rep rows 1–6 until work measures 20cm from cast on edge.
Cast off.

PATTERN 3:
TRICOLOUR FLAT RIB
Make 4 in Oats (mc), Apple (cc) and Bottle (cc2).
Cast on 41sts.
Row 1 (rs): mc knit.
Row 2: cc k2, [p2, k3] to last 4sts, p2, k2.
Row 3: cc2 knit.
Row 4: mc k2, [p2, k3] to last 4sts, p2, k2.
Row 5: cc knit.
Row 6: cc2 k2, [p2, k3] to last 4sts, p2, k2.
Rep rows 1–6, carrying the yarns not in use up the side, until work measures 20cm from cast on edge.
Cast off.

PATTERN 4:
TWISTED RIB
Make 2 in Apple and 2 in Bottle.
Cast on 42sts.
Row 1 (rs): knit.
Row 2: [p2, k2] to last 2sts, p2.
Row 3: k2, [p2, T.2] to last 4sts, p2, k2.
Row 4: purl.
Rep rows 1–4 until work measures 20cm from cast on edge.
Cast off.

TO MAKE UP
Block all the squares to the same size.
The blanket is 4 squares by 4 squares. To create the arrangement shown, sew them together using mattress stitch in the foll sequence:

Row 1
Pattern 3 : Pattern 2 : Pattern 1 : Pattern 4 in Bottle.
Row 2
Pattern 1 : Pattern 3 : Pattern 4 in Apple : Pattern 2.
Row 3
Pattern 2 : Pattern 4 in Apple : Pattern 3 : Pattern 1.
Row 4
Pattern 4 in Bottle : Pattern 1 : Pattern 2 : Pattern 3.

Then sew these rows together.

Patterns used in jumpers
Pattern 1 is used to make Pippin's Perfectly Pretty Coat, see page 32.
Pattern 2 is used to make Archie's Lovely Luxurious Jumper, see page 76.
Pattern 4 is used to make Bruno's Toasty Twisted Rib Jumper, see page 26.

 FACT FILE

SCOUT, AKA

SCOUTY-PANTS

Breed: Whippet.
Character: A gentle and loyal chap, Scout is chilled and will go with the flow.
Happiest When: Chasing a ball or Frisbee, or having tummy rubs.
Will Do Anything For: A ball.
Naughtiest Habit: His owner reports that he is perfect and has no naughty habits!
Favourite Treat: Food; if pushed for specifics, cheese.
Hobbies Include: Posing for his photographer owner even when there is no camera, chasing balls and sleeping in a luxurious jumper.

Scout's Super-Snugly Jumper

A cross between a coat and a jumper, this is knitted in a beautifully soft yarn for a touch of luxury. It has a moss stitch edge and a cable design to keep the knitter interested. The shaping is perfect for the curves of the whippet body and the long neck will keep out chilly draughts.

Size
Dog measurements
Neck 26–32cm
Shoulder 19–22cm
Chest 60–72cm
Length 54–58cm
See Measure Your Dog
(page 95)

Garment measurements
Neck 29cm unstretched
Chest 60cm unstretched
Length 51cm plus collar

Yarn
3 x 50g balls of Yarn Stories Fine Merino & Baby Alpaca Aran in Toffee (mc) and 1 x 50g ball in Taupe (cc)

Needles and equipment
Pair each of 3.5mm and 4mm knitting needles
Cable needle
8 safety pins to use as markers for leg holes
1 stitch holder
Knitter's sewing needle

Tension
23sts and 31 rows over st st to a 10cm square using 4mm needles.
The central cable and moss st panel is 11.5cm wide.

Abbreviations
See page 94.

Notes
This jumper is knitted from the neck down, and the top panel and under panel are divided at the bottom of the neck rib and worked separately.

TOP PANEL
With cc and 3.5mm needles, cast on 70sts.
Next row (rs): knit.
Next row: purl.
Change to mc.
Next row: knit.
Set rib patt
Next row (ws): [k1, p3] to last 2sts, k2.
Next row: k1, p1, [k3, p1] to end.
These 2 rows set rib patt. Cont in patt until rib measures 11cm from cast on edge, ending with a ws row. Cut yarn.
Change to 4mm needles.
Divide sts to form under panel sts and top panel sts by putting the first 26sts onto a stitch holder for the under panel. Rejoin yarn

43

and work rem 44sts of top panel as folls:

Row 1 (rs): p1, [k1, p1] twice, k2, p1, k1, p1, [k6, p1, k1, p1] 3 times, k2, p1, [k1, p1] twice.

Row 2: p1, [k1, p1] twice, p3, k1, p1, [p6, p1, k1, p1] 3 times, p3, [k1, p1] twice.

Row 3 (cable & inc row): p1, [k1, p1] twice, k2, M1, p1, k1, p1, [k2, C4F, p1, k1, p1] 3 times, M1, k2, p1, [k1, p1] twice. *(46sts)*

Row 4: p1, [k1, p1] twice, p4, k1, p1, [p6, p1, k1, p1] 3 times, p4, [k1, p1] twice.

Row 5: p1, [k1, p1] twice, k3, p1, k1, p1, [k6, p1, k1, p1] 3 times, k3, p1, [k1, p1] twice.

Row 6: p1, [k1, p1] twice, p4, k1, p1, [p6, p1, k1, p1] 3 times, p4, [k1, p1] twice.

Row 7 (cable & inc row): p1, [k1, p1] twice, k3, M1, p1, k1, p1, [C4B, k2, p1, k1, p1] 3 times, M1, k3, p1, [k1, p1] twice. *(48sts)*

Row 8: p1, [k1, p1] twice, p5, k1, p1, [p6, p1, k1, p1] 3 times, p5, [k1, p1] twice.

These 8 rows set central cable and moss st patt panel with border edges of st st and 5 moss sts.

Cont in patt, inc and work into st st at outer edge of central panel on every 4th row as set until there are 60sts, at same time, when work measures 11cm from bottom of neck rib, place a marker at each end of row to mark top of leg hole.

Now inc as before but on every rs row until there are 84sts, at same time, when work measures 10cm from first markers, place a marker at each end of row to mark bottom of leg hole.

Cont as set straight for a further 12cm, ending on a ws row, then start to dec.

Next row (dec row): patt to 2sts before central cable and moss st patt panel, k2tog, patt 30, k2togtbl, patt to end. *(82sts)*

Next row: Patt to end.

Rep last 2 rows until there are 66sts.

Cont straight in patt until panel measures 45cm from bottom of neck rib, ending with a ws row, dec 1st in centre of last row. *(65sts)*

Moss stitch border

Change to 3.5mm needles.

Next row (rs): k1, [p1, k1] to end.
Rep last row until the border measures 6cm, ending with a ws row.
Change to cc.
Beg with a k row, work 3 rows st st.
Cast off on ws.

UNDER PANEL

Rejoin cc to 26sts on stitch holder at bottom of neck rib.

Next row (inc row) (rs): k1, [p1, k1] twice, [p1, k3] 4 times, p1, M1, [p1, k1] twice. *(27sts)*

Next row: [k1, p1] twice, k1, [k1, p3] 4 times, k2, [p1, k1] twice.
This sets 17st central panel in k3, p1 rib with moss st border edges.

Shape chest

Next row (inc row): [k1, p1] twice, k1, M1, p1, [k3, p1] 4 times, M1, k1, [p1, k1] twice. *(29sts)*

Next row: [k1, p1] twice, k1, p1, [k1, p3] 4 times, k1, p1, k1, [p1, k1] twice.

Next row (inc row): [k1, p1]

TOP PANEL

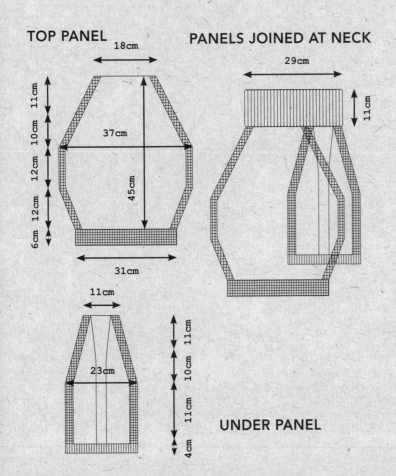

PANELS JOINED AT NECK

18cm
11cm
10cm
12cm
12cm
6cm
37cm
45cm
31cm

29cm
11cm

11cm
11cm
10cm
11cm
4cm
23cm

UNDER PANEL

twice, k2, M1, p1, [k3, p1] 4 times, M1, k2, [p1, k1] twice. *(31sts)*

Next row: [k1, p1] twice, k1, p2, [k1, p3] 4 times, k1, p2, k1, [p1, k2] twice.

Cont to inc and work into st st in this way at outer edges of central panel as set on every rs row until there are 53sts.

Cont in patt as set without shaping until work measures 11cm from bottom of neck rib. Place a marker at each end of row to mark top of leg hole. Cont in patt as set for 10cm. Place a marker at each end of row to mark bottom of leg hole. Cont in patt as set for 11cm, ending with a ws row.

Rib border
Change to 3.5mm needles.
Next row (dec row) (rs): k3, p1, [k1, k2tog, k1, p1] 3 times, [k3, p1] 4 times, [k1, k2tog, k1, p1] 3 times, k3. *(47sts)*

Next row: k1, p2, k1, [p3, k1] 10 times, p2, k1.
Next row: p1, k2, p1, [k3, p1] 10 times, k2, p1.
Rep last 2 rows until rib measures 4cm, and panel measures 36cm from bottom of neck rib.
Cast off loosely in patt.

TO MAKE UP
Block both panels gently, so as not to flatten the cable or rib. Sew up both shoulder seams from the top leg marker to the neck rib. Join neck rib seam. Then sew the side seams from the bottom leg marker to the bottom of the under panel, which should line up with the start of the final shaping on the top panel.
Weave in all loose ends.

☸ FACT FILE

DYLAN
....

Breed: Miniature Wire-Haired Dachshund.

Character: Gentle, kind and contented. He was rescued when he was just 6 months old, emaciated and dehydrated but with love and care he now enjoys a full and happy life.

Happiest When: Digging for his ball!

Will Do Anything For: Food.

Naughtiest Habit: Placing his ball under the kitchen units and talking non-stop at 5pm every day!

Favourite Treat: Freshly dug-up organic carrots.

Hobbies Include: Sleeping, eating and ball-hiding.

Dylan's Dandy Rib Dog Jumper

You produce this lovely stitch pattern by just purling every stitch on wrong side rows; it looks great on the reverse too, where the neck is turned back. The jumper has little garter stitch leg holes so it is more of a tank top and is ideal for short legs that love to dig.

Size
Dog measurements
Neck 22–28cm
Shoulder 12–15cm
Chest 38–44cm
Length 35–39cm
See Measure Your Dog
  (page 95)

Garment measurements
Neck 24cm unstretched
Chest 43cm unstretched
Length 33cm plus collar

Yarn
2 x 100g ball of Rowan Pure Wool
  Worsted in Grasshopper 130

Needles and equipment
Pair each of 4mm and 4.5mm
  knitting needles
6 safety pins to use as markers
  for leg holes
1 stitch holder
Knitter's sewing needle

Tension
22sts and 30 rows over patt to
  a 10cm square using 4.5mm
  needles.

Abbreviations
See page 94.

JUMPER
Starting at the neck edge and with 4mm needles, cast on 54sts.
Set rib patt
Row 1 (rs): [k2, p2] to last 2sts, k2.
Row 2: purl.
These 2 rows set rib patt. Cont in patt until rib measures 9cm from cast on edge, ending with a ws row.
Change to 4.5mm needles.
Next row (inc row): k1, M1, k1, [p2, k1, M1, k1] to end. (*68sts*)
Next row: purl.
Next row: [k3, p2] to last 3sts, k3.
Next row: purl.
The last 2 rows set new rib patt. Cont in patt until rib measures 15cm from cast on edge, ending with a ws row.
Place a marker on each edge at this point to mark top of leg shaping. Cut yarn.
Divide sts to form under panel sts and top panel sts by putting the first 20sts onto a stitch holder

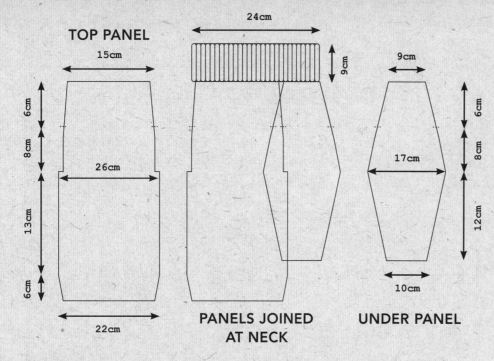

TOP PANEL

15cm

6cm

8cm

26cm

13cm

22cm

6cm

PANELS JOINED AT NECK

24cm

9cm

UNDER PANEL

9cm

17cm

10cm

6cm

8cm

12cm

and work on the 48sts for the top panel. Rejoin yarn.

Next row (inc row): k1, M1, k2, [p2, k1, M1, k2] to end. *(58sts)*

Next row: purl.

Next row: [k4, p2] to last 4sts, k4.

Next row: purl.

The last 2 rows set new rib patt. Cont in patt until rib measures 8cm from where it was divided. Place a marker on each edge at this point to mark start of leg hole.

Cont in patt as set until work

measures 36cm from cast on edge, ending with a ws row.

Shape rump

Next row (rs): work 29sts, place a marker to mark the centre, work 29sts.

Next row: purl, slm, purl to end.

Next row (dec row): [k4, p2] 4 times, k3, k2tog, slm, k2tog, k3, [p2, k4] 4 times. *(56sts)*

Next row: purl, slm.

Cont to dec as set by last 2 rows (working k2tog on either side of the marker on every rs row) 7 times more. *(42sts)*

Work measures 42cm from cast on edge, ending with a ws row. Knit one row.
Cast off knitwise on ws.

UNDER PANEL

With rs facing, rejoin yarn to 20sts on stitch holder.

Next row (inc row) (rs): k2, M1, k1, [p2, k3] 3 times, k2tog. *(20sts)*

Next row: purl.

Next row (inc row): k2, M1, k2, [p2, k3] twice, p2, k2, M1, k2. *(22sts)*

Next row: purl.

Cont to inc and work into st st on every rs row inside edge sts as set until there are 38sts.

Place marker at each end of row to mark bottom of leg hole.

Next row (dec row) (rs): k2, k2tog, k9, [p2, k3] twice, p2, k9, k2tog, k2.

Next row: purl.

Cont to dec on every rs row inside edge sts as set until there are 20sts.

Next row (rs): k4, p2, k3, p2, k3, p2, k4.

Next row: purl.

The last 2 rows set rib patt. Cont in patt until work measures 35cm

from cast on edge, ending with a ws row.
Knit one row.
Cast off knitwise on ws.

TO MAKE UP
Sew the under panel to the top panel from the neck to the first marker at top of leg hole shaping.

Leg hole border
With 4.5mm needles and rs facing, pick up 30sts along the top panel from the second marker at start of leg hole up to the seam and along the same point on the under panel.
Knit one row.
Cast off knitwise.
Work the second leg to match.
Sew up the side seams from the legs down.
Weave in all loose ends.

🐾 FACT FILE

NELLY
....

Breed: Miniature Schnauzer.
Character: Always on the go;
always pleased to see anyone!
Happiest When: Playing with
her constant companion,
Isabella (aged 5) and going
for long walks.
Will Do Anything For:
Food – any kind of food.
Hobbies Include: Chasing
cats, sliding down the
slide into the paddling
pool (summer only) and
trampolining.
Favourite Treat: Dried
venison bites.

Nelly's Properly Practical Coat

The item that inspired this terrier coat was a vintage Aran jumper bought in a French flea market. I enjoyed the challenge of knitting the trellis pattern. The shape is kept simple with a triangle under panel that helps the coat fit well and stay in place.

Size
Dog measurements
Neck 26–34cm
Shoulder 16–20cm
Chest 54–66cm
Length 41cm
See Measure your Dog
  (page 95)

Garment measurements
Neck 32cm unstretched
Chest 52cm unstretched
Length 38cm plus collar

Yarn
2 x 100g balls of Rowan Pure
  Wool Worsted in Raspberry 117

Needles and equipment
Pair each of 4.5mm and 5mm
  knitting needles
Cable needle
2 stitch markers
Knitter's sewing needle

Tension
25sts and 27 rows over patt
  to a 10cm square using
  5mm needles.
The central panel is 12cm wide.

Abbreviations
See page 94.

TOP PANEL
Starting at the lower edge and with 4.5mm needles, cast on 89sts.
Row 1 (rs): [k1, p3] to last st, k1.
Row 2: [p1, k3] to last st, p1.
These 2 rows set rib patt. Cont in patt until rib measures 4cm from cast on edge, ending with a ws row.
Change to 5mm needles.
Set border patt and central panel
Next row (dec row) (rs): k2tog, [p1, k1] 3 times, [Tw2, p4] 3 times, Tw2, place marker, p2, k30, p2, place marker, Tw2, [p4, Tw2] 3 times, [k1, p1] 3 times, k1. *(88sts)*
Next row: k1, [p1, k1] 3 times, [p2, k4] 3 times, p2, slm, k2, p30, k2, slm, p2, [k4, p2] 3 times, [k1, p1] 3 times, k1.
Set trellis pattern into central panel
Row 1 (rs): k1, [p1, k1] 3 times, [Tw2, p4] 3 times, Tw2, slm, p2,

[Cr2f, p4, Cr1b] 3 times, p2, slm, Tw2, [p4, Tw2] 3 times, [k1, p1] 3 times, k1.

Row 2: k1, [p1, k1] 3 times, [p2, k4] 3 times, p2, slm, k3, [p2, k4, p2, k2] 3 times, k1, slm, p2, [k4, p2] 3 times, [k1, p1] 3 times, k1.

Row 3: k1, [p1, k1] 3 times, [Tw2, p4] 3 times, Tw2, slm, p3, [Cr2f, p2, Cr1b, p2] 3 times, p1, slm, Tw2, [p4, Tw2] 3 times, [k1, p1] 3 times, k1.

Row 4: k1, [p1, k1] 3 times, [p2, k4] 3 times, p2, slm, [k4, p2, k2, p2] 3 times, k4, slm, p2, [k4, p2] 3 times, [k1, p1] 3 times, k1.

Row 5: k1, [p1, k1] 3 times, [Tw2, p4] 3 times, Tw2, slm, [p4, Cr2f, Cr1b] 3 times, p4, slm, Tw2, [p4, Tw2] 3 times, [k1, p1] 3 times, k1.

Row 6: k1, [p1, k1] 3 times, [p2, k4] 3 times, p2, slm, [k5, p4, k1] 3 times, k4, slm, p2, [k4, p2] 3 times, [k1, p1] 3 times, k1.

Row 7: k1, [p1, k1] 3 times, [Tw2, p4] 3 times, Tw2, slm, [p5, C4B, p1] 3 times, p4, slm, Tw2, [p4, Tw2] 3 times, [k1, p1] 3 times, k1.

Row 8: k1, [p1, k1] 3 times, [p2, k4] 3 times, p2, slm, [k5, p4, k1] 3 times, k4, slm, p2, [k4, p2] 3 times, [k1, p1] 3 times, k1.

Row 9: k1, [p1, k1] 3 times, [Tw2, p4] 3 times, Tw2, slm, [p4, Cr1b, Cr2f] 3 times, p4, slm, Tw2, [p4, Tw2] 3 times, [k1, p1] 3 times, k1.

Row 10: k1, [p1, k1] 3 times, [p2, k4] 3 times, p2, slm, [k4, p2, k2, p2] 3 times, k4, slm, p2, [k4, p2] 3 times, [k1, p1] 3 times, k1.

Row 11: k1, [p1, k1] 3 times, [Tw2, p4] 3 times, Tw2, slm, p3, [Cr1b, p2, Cr2f, p2] 3 times, p1, slm, Tw2, [p4, Tw2] 3 times, [k1, p1] 3 times, k1.

Row 12: k1, [p1, k1] 3 times, [p2, k4] 3 times, p2, slm, k3, [p2, k4, p2, k2] 3 times, k1, slm, p2, [k4, p2] 3 times, [k1, p1] 3 times, k1.

Row 13: k1, [p1, k1] 3 times, [Tw2, p4] 3 times, Tw2, slm, p2, [Cr1b, p4, Cr2f] 3 times, p2, slm, Tw2, [p4, Tw2] 3 times, [k1, p1] 3 times, k1.

Row 14: k1, [p1, k1] 3 times, [p2, k4] 3 times, p2, slm, k2, [p2, k6, p2] 3 times, k2, slm, p2, [k4, p2] 3 times, [k1, p1] 3 times, k1.

Row 15: k1, [p1, k1] 3 times, [Tw2, p4] 3 times, Tw2, slm, p2, k2, [p6, C4F] twice, p6, k2, p2, slm, Tw2, [p4, Tw2] 3 times, [k1, p1] 3 times, k1.

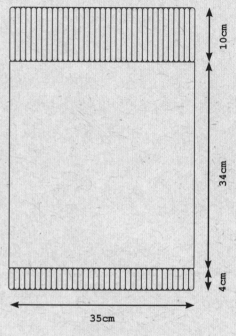

TOP PANEL

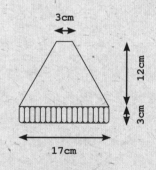

UNDER PANEL

Row 16: k1, [p1, k1] 3 times, [p2, k4] 3 times, p2, slm, k2, [p2, k6, p2] 3 times, k2, slm, p2, [k4, p2] 3 times, [k1, p1] 3 times, k1. These 16 rows set trellis patt in central panel. Cont in patt until work measures approximately 38cm from cast on edge, ending with either row 8 or row 16 of patt rep.

Neck rib
Change to 4.5mm needles.
Next row (dec row) (rs): [k3, p1] to last 4sts, k2, k2tog. *(87sts)*
Next row: [p3, k1] to last 3sts, p3.
Next row: [k3, p1] to last 3sts, k3.
The last 2 rows set rib patt. Cont in patt until rib measures 10cm, then cast off loosely in patt. Sew the neck seam, starting on the rs, then turning to the ws halfway down so that the seam does not show when the neck is rolled down.

UNDER PANEL
With 4.5mm needles and rs of body facing, pick up 7sts across bottom of neck seam, starting 1cm down from seam on one side and picking up across to 1cm down on the other side.

Next row: k1, p5, k1
Next row: knit.
Next row: k1, p5, k1.
Change to 5mm needles.
Next row (inc row) (rs): k2, M1, k3, M1, k2. *(9sts)*
Next row: k1, p7, k1.
The last 2 rows set incs in patt. Cont to inc as set until there are 37sts, ending with a ws row.
Rib border
Next row: [k1, p3] to last st, k1.
Next row: [p1, k3] to last st, p1.
The last 2 rows set rib patt. Cont in patt until rib measures 3cm, then cast off loosely in patt.

TO MAKE UP
Block both panels gently. Right sides together, fold the under panel flat against the top panel and, starting at the cast off edge of the under panel, sew each end of the rib section to the sides of the top panel.

 FACT FILE

FRANKIE

Breed: Lurcher (Whippet/Saluki cross).

Character: Gentle, kind and loved by all. Scared of her own shadow and anything that makes a loud bang.

Happiest When: Chasing squirrels.

Will Do Anything For: Venison chews.

Naughtiest Habit: Creeping upstairs after lights out and messing up the spare bed to get comfy for the night.

Favourite Treat: Chicken, freshly roasted.

Hobbies Include: Sleeping, begging for toast and barking at cats.

Frankie's Super Sloppy Joe Jumper

I love knitting in the round because you are always looking at the right side, there are very few seams to sew up and it really isn't difficult to do. The double moss stitch pattern looks great in this Aran-weight yarn and the shaping gives this jumper a lovely fit around the neck and shoulders.

Size
Dog measurements
Neck 36–40cm
Shoulder 28cm
Chest 71–75cm
Length 66–69cm
See Measure Your Dog
  (page 95)

Garment measurements
Neck 30cm unstretched
Chest 69cm unstretched
Length 61cm plus collar

Yarn
4 x 100g balls of Wendy
  Traditional Aran in Grouse 191

Needles and equipment
One each of 4mm and 5mm
  circular needles
Set of 4 x 4mm double-pointed
  needles
4 stitch markers
3 stitch holders
Knitter's sewing needle

Tension
18sts and 28 rows over double
  moss patt to a 10cm square
  using 5mm needles.

Abbreviations
See page 94.

Notes
This jumper is knitted for the
  most part in the round on a
  circular needle, and the pattern
  assumes that the rs is the inside
  of the knitting.

JUMPER
Starting at the neck edge and with 4mm circular needle, cast on 72sts. Ensuring that the work is not twisted, place marker and join the round.
Round 1: [k2, p2] to end.
This row sets rib patt. Cont in patt until rib measures 2cm, then change to 5mm circular needle and cont until rib measures 15cm (or length of dog's neck) from cast on edge.
Divide sts to form back sts, first leg sts, chest sts and second leg sts as folls:
Next round: working in k2, p2, rib throughout, rib across 22sts for back, place marker, rib across

18sts for first leg, place marker, rib across 14sts for chest, place marker, rib across 18sts for second leg.

Set double moss back panel and rib patt

Next round: [k2, p2] across back sts to last 2sts, k2, slm, rib as set across first leg, chest and second leg sts, slm.

Next round: [k2, p2] across back sts to last 2sts, k2, slm, rib as set across first leg, chest and second leg sts, slm.

Next round: [p2, k2] across back sts to last 2sts, p2, slm, rib as set across first leg, chest and second leg sts, slm.

Next round: [p2, k2] across back sts to last 2sts, p2, slm, rib as set across first leg, chest and second leg sts, slm.

Shape shoulder

Next round (inc round): k1, M1, k1, [p2, k2] across back sts to last 4sts, p2, k1, M1, k1, slm, rib as set across first leg, chest and second leg sts, slm.

Inc back sts on every round in this way (working 1st in patt, making a stitch, working in patt to 1st before marker, making a stitch,

working last st in patt), taking incs into double moss patt, until there are 92sts on the back panel (35 inc rounds worked).
Cont in patt with no further incs until work measures 19cm from the bottom of rib: check that from centre back neck diagonally down to edge measures 28cm (dog's shoulder length).

Make leg holes
Next round: work back sts in patt, rib across 18 first leg sts then put them onto a stitch holder, rib across 14 chest sts, rib across 18 second leg sts then put them onto a stitch holder.
Next round: work back sts in patt, cast on 18sts for first leg, rib across 14 chest sts, cast on

18sts for second leg, ensuring the markers are in place again. Cont to knit in the round in patt as set until work measures 43cm from bottom of neck rib.
Shape under chest
Next round (dec round): work back sts in patt, rib across first leg sts to 1st before marker, slip next st onto rh needle, remove

BACK

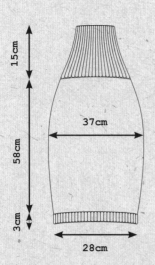

15cm

58cm

3cm

37cm

28cm

FRONT

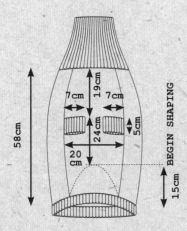

58cm

7cm 19cm 7cm

24cm

20 cm

5cm

BEGIN SHAPING

1.5cm

marker and slip st back onto lh needle, k2tog, rib across chest sts to 1st before marker, slip next st onto rh needle, remove marker and slip st back onto lh needle, k2tog, rib across second leg sts. Cont to dec as set on every round, altering the dec made (either k2tog or p2tog) to suit patt, until all 18sts of each leg are eliminated. Under panel should now measure approximately 48cm from bottom of neck rib.

Next round: work back sts in patt as set, rib across 14 chest sts then put them onto a stitch holder. Work back sts, working back and forth on the circular needle.

Shape rump

Next row (dec row) (rs): k2, k2tog, work in patt as set to last 4sts, k2tog, k2.

Next row: work in patt as set. Cont to dec as set on every rs row, working the dec 2sts in from the edge, altering the dec made (k2tog or p2tog) to suit patt, until you have 68sts and the work measures approximately 58cm.

Rib border

Turn work to rs out. With rs facing and 4mm circular needle, knit in

pattern across the back 68sts, then pick up 19sts down the first side, knit across the 14 chest sts, then pick up 19sts down the other side of the top panel to complete the round.

Place marker and commence working in the round.

Next round: [k2, p2] to end.

Rep last round 5 times more.

Cast off loosely in patt.

LEG HOLE BORDER

With rs facing and 4mm dpns, pick up 18sts along cast off edge of leg hole, then rib the 18sts from the stitch holder.

Place a marker at beg of round.

Round 1: [k2, p2] to end.

Rep this round 11 times more.

Cast off loosely in patt.

Repeat for second leg hole border.

TO MAKE UP

Weave in all loose ends.

🐾 FACT FILE

RALPH
....

Breed: Long-Haired Chihuahua.

Character: Confident, happy chap with a big ego; he knows how handsome he is!

Happiest When: Running around with his buddies.

Will Do Anything For: A bit of flattery.

Naughtiest Habit: Sneaking under the duvet.

Favourite Treat: Scrambled egg.

Hobbies Include: Chasing Lottie the Jack Russell and Ruby the Collie Lurcher.

Ralph's Marvellous Multi-Coloured Jumper

I had fun with this multi-coloured yarn by using two strands held together. The vibrant result looks best in stocking stitch, making this a great project for a beginner knitter. Don't be put off by having to use two strands of yarn; you'll quickly get used to handling them.

Size
Dog measurements
Neck 16–20cm
Shoulder 10–14cm
Chest 32–38cm
Length 30–33cm
See Measure Your Dog
  (page 95)

Garment measurements
Neck 19cm unstretched
Chest 29cm unstretched
Length 29cm plus collar

Yarn
2 x 50g balls of Louisa Harding
  Amitola in Dark Rose 111

Needles and equipment
Pair of 4mm knitting needles
4 safety pins to use as markers
  for leg holes
1 stitch holder
Knitter's sewing needle

Tension
24sts and 34 rows over st st to
  a 10cm square using 4mm
  needles and two strands of
  yarn held together.

Abbreviations
See page 94.

TOP PANEL
Starting at the lower edge and with 4mm needles and one strand of yarn from each ball held together, cast on 42sts.
Row 1 (rs): k4, [p2, k2] to last 6sts, p2, k4.
Row 2: k2, [p2, k2] to end.
These 2 rows set rib patt.
Rep rows 1–2, 4 times more.
Beg with a k row, work 10 rows st st.
Shape rump
Next row (inc row) (rs): k2, M1, k to last 2sts, M1, k2. *(44sts)*
Inc on every 4th row until there are 56sts.
Cont in st st without shaping until work measures 18cm from cast on edge.
Shape leg
Next row (rs): cast off 3sts, k to end. *(53sts)*
Next row: Cast off 3sts, p to end. *(50sts)*

Next row (dec row): k2, k2tog, k to last 4sts, k2tog, k2. *(48sts)*
Next row: purl.
Next row (dec row): k2, k2tog, k to last 4sts, k2tog, k2. *(46sts)*
Cont in st st without shaping until leg hole measures 5cm. Place a marker at each end of row to mark top of leg hole.
Cont in st st without shaping until work measures 25cm from cast on edge, ending with a ws row.
Shape shoulder
Next row (dec row) (rs): k2, k2tog, k to last 4sts, k2tog, k2. *(44sts)*
Cont to dec as set on every rs row until there are 38sts, finishing with a ws row.
Cont without shaping until work measures 29cm from cast on edge, then put these 38sts onto a stitch holder and block this panel.

UNDER PANEL
Starting at the lower edge and with 4mm needles and one strand of yarn from each ball held together, cast on 24sts.
Row 1: k3, [p2, k2] to last 5sts, p2, k3.
Row 2: k1, p2, [k2, p2] to last 5sts, k2, p2, k1.

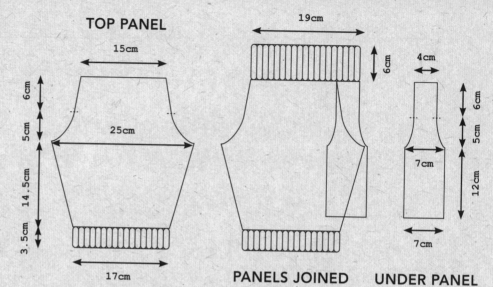

TOP PANEL
15cm
6cm
5cm
25cm
14.5cm
3.5cm
17cm

19cm
6cm

PANELS JOINED AT NECK

4cm
6cm
7cm
5cm
12cm
7cm

UNDER PANEL

These 2 rows set rib patt. Cont in patt until rib measures 12cm from cast on edge, ending with a ws row.
Shape leg
Next row (rs): cast off 3sts, patt to end. *(21sts)*
Next row: cast off 3sts, patt to end. *(18sts)*
Next row (dec row): patt 2, k2tog, patt to last 4sts, k2tog, patt 2. *(16sts)*
Cont to dec as set on every alt rs row, altering the dec made (either k2tog or p2tog) to suit patt until there are 12sts.

Cont in patt as set without shaping until leg hole measures 5cm. Place marker at each end of row to mark top of leg hole.
Cont in st st without shaping until work matches top panel from top of leg hole, ending with a ws row.
Join neck
Next row (rs): k1, [p2, k2] twice, p2, k1, work across 38sts of top panel on stitch holder, k1, [p2, k2] to last 5sts, p2, k3.
Next row: starting with p3 and ending with p1, knit the knits and purl the purls in patt.

Cont in patt as set for 6cm.
Cast off loosely in patt.

TO MAKE UP
Join the shoulder seams down
to marker.

With rs facing and 4mm needles,
pick up 24sts along the leg hole,
from the leg shaping on the top
panel, up to the shoulder seam
and down to the start of the leg
shaping on the under panel. It
doesn't matter if you pick up
more stitches, but do not pick
up fewer, and ensure you have
a number divisible by 4.

Set rib patt
Next row (ws): [k2, p2] to end.
Next row: [p2, k2] to end.
Rep last 2 rows, then rep first row
once more.
Cast off loosely in patt.
Work the second leg to match.
Sew up the leg seams and then
sew the top panel to the under
panel.
Weave in all loose ends.

🐾 FACT FILE

EDIE
....

Breed: Bedlington Terrier.
Character: Funny, happy, inquisitive little dog; very easily distracted!
Happiest When: She has an audience!
Will Do Anything For: Dried fish skins.
Naughtiest Habit: Barking at dogs on the television.
Favourite Treat: Prawn crackers and sausages.
Hobbies Include: Watching tennis and noisily dropping her toys from the sofa onto the floor.

Edie's Robust Romp-Around Jumper

This stitch pattern is so easy to work; it is just a simple combination of knits and purls, yet will leave the knitter feeling as though they have really achieved something special. I have chosen two colours that are perfect for Edie, but the texture would work well with just one colour.

Size
Dog measurements
Neck 26–34cm
Shoulder 16–20cm
Chest 54–66cm
Length 48–51cm
See Measure Your Dog
  (page 95)

Garment measurements
Neck 24cm unstretched
Chest 52cm unstretched
Length 44cm plus collar

Yarn
2 x 50g skeins of Erika Knight
  Vintage Wool in Drizzle (mc)
  and 1 x 50g skein in Flax (cc)

Needles and equipment
Pair each of 4mm and 4.5mm
  knitting needles
4 safety pins to use as markers
  for leg holes
1 stitch holder
Knitter's sewing needle

Tension
19sts and 30 rows over ridge and
  stripe patt to a 10cm square
  using 4.5mm needles.

Abbreviations
See page 94.

TOP PANEL
Starting at the lower edge and with 4mm needles and cc, cast on 54sts.
Row 1 (rs): k4, [p2, k2] to last 6sts, p2, k4.
Row 2: k2, [p2, k2] to end.
These 2 rows set rib patt.
Change to mc.
Rep last 2 rows 5 times more, dec 1st at beg of last row. *(53sts)*
Change to 4.5mm needles.
Change to cc.
Row 1 (rs): knit.
Row 2: k1, p to last st, k1.
Change to mc.
Row 3: knit.
Row 4: k1, p to last st, k1.
Row 5: knit.
Row 6: k1, p to last st, k1.
Row 7: k1, p to last st, k1.
Row 8: k1, [p1, k1] to end.
These 8 rows form ridge and stripe patt, which is repeated throughout the panel.

Shape rump

Next row (inc row): k2, M1, k to last 2sts, M1, k2. *(55sts)*
Work rows 2–4 of patt.
Next row (inc row): k2, M1, k to last 2sts, M1, k2. *(57sts)*
Work rows 6–8 of patt.
Cont in patt, increasing on rows 1 and 5 as set, until there are 65sts.
Cont in patt without shaping until work measures 25cm from cast on edge, ending with row 8 of patt.

Shape leg

Keeping ridge and stripe patt correct:
Next row: cast off 4sts, k to end. *(61sts)*
Next row: cast off 4sts, p to last st, k1. *(57sts)*
Next row (dec row): k2, k2tog, k to last 4sts, k2tog, k2. *(55sts)*
Next row: k1, p to last st, k1.
Work rows 5–8 of patt.
Next row (dec row): k2, k2tog, k to last 4sts, k2tog, k2. *(53sts)*
Work rows 2–4 of patt.
Next row (dec row): k2, k2tog, k to last 4sts, k2tog, k2. *(51sts)*
Work rows 6–8 of patt.
Cont in patt without shaping until work measures approximately 34cm from cast on edge, ending

with row 2, 4 or 8 of patt, at the same time leg hole measures 9cm from start of shaping, place marker at each end of row to mark top of leg hole.

Shape shoulder

Next row (dec row) (rs): k2, k2tog, k to last 4sts, k2tog, k2. *(49sts)*
Next row: k1, p to last st, k1.
Cont to dec on every 4th row until there are 45sts. Cont in patt until panel measures 44cm from cast on edge, ending with row 2 of patt, dec 1st in centre of last

row. Put these 44sts onto a stitch holder and set aside.

UNDER PANEL

Starting at the lower edge and with 4.5mm needles and mc, cast on 36sts.
Row 1 (rs): k3, [p2, k2] to last 5sts, p2, k3.
Row 2: k1, p2, [k2, p2] to last 5sts, k2, p2, k1.
These 2 rows set rib patt. Cont in patt until rib measures 2cm from cast on edge, ending with a ws row.

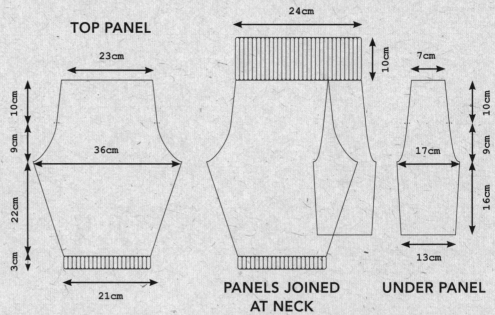

TOP PANEL

23cm

10cm

9cm

36cm

22cm

3cm

21cm

24cm

10cm

PANELS JOINED AT NECK

7cm

10cm

17cm

9cm

16cm

13cm

UNDER PANEL

Shape tummy

Next row (inc row) (rs): k2, M1, k1, [p2, k2] to last 5sts, p2, k1, M1, k2. *(38sts)*

Next row: k1, p3, [k2, p2] to last 6sts, k2, p3, k1.

Keeping 2 edge sts as st st, cont in patt, inc on every 4th row as set until there are 48sts. Knit the first and last stitch on ws rows to give a neat edge.

Cont without shaping until work measures 16cm from cast on edge, ending with a ws row.

Shape leg

Next row (rs): cast off 6sts, patt to end. *(42sts)*

Next row: cast off 6sts, patt to end. *(36sts)*

Next row (dec row): k2, k2tog, patt to last 4sts, k2tog, k2. *(34sts)*

Next row: k1, patt to last st, k1.

Keeping patt as set, dec on next and every 4th rs row until there are 26sts.

Place a marker at each end of the row when leg hole measures 9cm from start of shaping.

Cont straight until work matches top panel from leg hole marker, ending with a ws row.

Join the neck

With mc and rs facing on under panel, [k2, p2] 6 times, k2 across these 26sts, then with rs facing cont the rib as set across the 44sts of the top panel on the stitch holder. *(70sts)*

Work in patt until rib measures 9cm.

Cut mc and join in cc.

Work 2 rows in patt.

Cast off loosely in patt.

TO MAKE UP

Sew up the shoulder seam from the bottom of the neck rib down to the markers at the top of the leg hole.

For the other shoulder seam, turn the work inside out, and starting at the neck edge and using mattress stitch, sew 5cm of the seam, then turn work back to right side and finish the seam down to the markers at the top of the leg hole.

Leg hole border

With rs facing, mc and 4mm needles, pick up 34sts along the leg hole, from the leg shaping on the top panel, up to the shoulder seam and down to the start of the leg shaping on the under panel. It doesn't matter if you pick up more stitches, but do not pick up fewer, and ensure you have a number divisible by 4 plus 2.

Set rib patt

Next row (ws): [p2, k2] to last 2sts, p2.

Next row: [k2, p2] to last 2sts, k2.

Rep last 2 rows 3 times more.

Cut mc and join in cc.

Work 2 rows in patt.

Cast off loosely in patt.

Work the second leg to match.

Sew up the leg seams and then sew the top panel to the under panel, noting that the under panel is shorter.

FACT FILE

ARCHIE
....

Breed: West Highland Terrier.
Character: A busy chap, always curious and happy. Loves to please his devoted owner.
Happiest When: On the pantomime stage doing his thing to the delight of an audience.
Will Do Anything For: Cheese.
Naughtiest Habit: Stubbornly refusing to leave the horse yard when he is not ready to go.
Favourite Treat: Chicken or a juicy bone.
Hobbies Include: Lazing by the fire, and waking the house up at silly o'clock to be tucked up in bed.

Archie's Lovely Luxurious Jumper

I love that a simple repeat can produce such a bold texture. There is an easy-to-work cable stitch on one row but all other rows are knits and purls, so this is a great jumper to try if you are new to knitting cables, though some concentration is needed to keep the pattern in line as you increase.

Size
Dog measurements
Neck 22–34cm
Shoulder 16–20cm
Chest 54–66cm
Length 44cm
See Measure Your Dog
  (page 95)

Garment measurements
Neck 23cm unstretched
Chest 50cm unstretched
Length 41cm plus collar

Yarn
3 x 50g balls of Yarn Stories
  Fine Merino & Baby Alpaca DK
  in Burnt Sienna

Needles and equipment
Pair each of 3.5mm and 4mm
  knitting needles
Cable needle
2 stitch markers
8 safety pins to use as markers
  for leg holes
1 stitch holder
Knitter's sewing needle

Tension
30sts and 31 rows over st st to
  a 10cm square using 4mm
  needles.

Abbreviations
See page 94.

JUMPER
Starting at the neck edge and with 3.5mm needles, cast on 78sts.
Knit one row.
Row 1 (ws): [k2tbl, p2] to last 2sts, k2tbl.
Row 2: k1, p1, [k2, p2] to last 2sts, p1, k1.
These 2 rows set rib patt.
Cont in patt until rib measures 5cm from cast on edge, ending with a rs row.
Next row (ws): [k2, p2] to last 2sts, k2.
Next row: k1, p1, [k2, p2] to last 2sts, p1, k1.
These 2 rows set new rib patt.
Cont in patt until whole rib section measures 10cm from cast on edge, ending with a ws row.
Change to 4mm needles.
Next row (rs): k1, p1, [k2, p2] 5 times, k2, p1, k1 (*26sts for under panel*), put these 26sts onto a stitch holder.

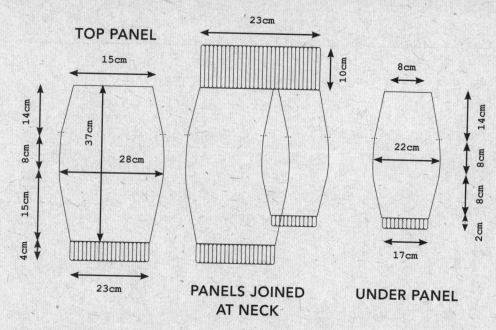

TOP PANEL

15cm

14cm

8cm

15cm

4cm

37cm

28cm

23cm

23cm

10cm

PANELS JOINED AT NECK

UNDER PANEL

8cm

22cm

14cm

8cm

8cm

2cm

17cm

Work rem 52sts for top panel.
Row 1 (rs): k1, p3, [k4, p4] to last 8sts, k4, p3, k1.
Row 2: [k4, p4] to last 4sts, k4.
Row 3: knit.
Row 4: k1, p to last st, k1.
Row 5: [k4, C4F] to last 4sts, k4.
Row 6: k1, p to last st, k1.
These 6 rows form cable patt.
Rep rows 1–6, 3 times more, then rep rows 1–2 once more.
Shape shoulder
Next row (inc row): k3, M1, k to last 3sts, M1, k3. (54sts)
Next row: k1, p to last st, k1.

Next row (inc row): k3, M1, k2, C4F, [k4, C4F] to last 5sts, k2, M1, k3. (56sts)
Next row: k1, p to last st, k1.
Next row: k1, p5, [k4, p4] to last 10sts, k4, p5, k1.
Next row: k6, [p4, k4] to last 10sts, p4, k6.
Next row (inc row): k3, M1, k to last 3sts, M1, k3. (58sts)
Next row: k1, p to last st, k1.
Next row (inc row): k3, M1, k4, [C4F, k4] to last 11sts, C4F, k4, M1, k3. (60sts)
Next row: k1, p to last st, k1.

Next row: k1, p7, [k4, p4] to last 12sts, k4, p7, k1.
Next row: k8, [p4, k4] to last 8sts, p4, k8.
Next row (inc row): k3, M1, k to last 3sts, M1, k3. (62sts)
Next row: k1, p to last st, k1.
Next row (inc row): k3, M1, k6, [C4F, k4] to last 13sts, C4F, k6, M1, k3. (64sts)
Next row: k1, p to last st, k1.
Next row: k1, p9, [k4, p4] to last 14sts, k4, p9, k1.
Next row: k10, [p4, k4] to last 14sts, p4, k10.
Next row (inc row): k3, M1, k to last 4sts, M1, k3. (66sts)
Next row: k1, p to last st, k1.
Next row (inc row): k3, M1, [C4F, k4] to last 7sts, C4F, M1, k3. (68sts)
Next row: k1, p to last st, k1.
Next row: k1, p3, [k4, p4] to last 8sts, k4, p3, k1.
Next row: k4, [p4, k4] to last 8sts, p4, k4.
Next row (inc row): k3, M1, k to last 4sts, M1, k3. (70sts)
Next row: k1, p to last st, k1.
Next row (inc row): k3, M1, k2, [C4F, p4] to last 9sts, C4F, k2, M1, k3. (72sts)

Row 3: knit.
Row 4: k1, p to last st, k1.
Row 5: k6, [C4F, p4] to last 10sts, C4F, k6.
Row 6: k1, p to last st, k1.
These 6 rows form new cable patt. Cont in patt until work measures 8cm from second marker, ending with patt row 2.

Shape rump
Next row (dec row) (row 3 of cable patt): k3, k2tog, k to last 5sts, k2tog, k3. *(70 sts)*
Cont to work cable patt as set, dec on every rs row and keeping the rest of the cable patt in line, until there are 54sts.
Cont in patt without shaping until work measures 37cm from bottom of neck rib, ending with patt row 6.

Rib border
Change to 3.5mm needles.
Row 1 (rs): k1, k1tbl, p2, [k2tbl, p2] to last 2sts, k1tbl, k1.
Row 2: k1, p1, [k2, p2] to last 4sts, k2, p1, k1.
These 2 rows set rib patt. Cont in patt until rib measures 4cm, then cast off loosely in patt.

Next row: k1, p to last st, k1.
Measure 14cm from bottom of neck rib and place a marker at each end of the row to mark the top of the leg hole.
Cont in 6-row cable patt with no further incs until leg hole measures 8cm, ending with patt row 6, then place another marker to mark bottom of leg hole.
Row 1 (rs): k1, p5, [k4, p4] to last 10sts, k4, p5, k1.
Row 2: k6, [p4, k4] to last 10sts, p4, k6.

UNDER PANEL

Put 26sts on stitch holder onto a 4mm needle and rejoin yarn.

Shape shoulder

Next row (inc row) (rs): k3, M1, k1, p2, [k2, p2] to last 4sts, k1, M1, k3. *(28sts)*

Next row: k1, p4, k2, [p2, k2] to last 5sts, p4, k1.

Next row (inc row): k3, M1, k2, p2, [k2, p2] to last 5sts, k2, M1, k3. *(30sts)*

Next row: k1, p5, k2, [p2, k2] to last 6sts, p5, k1.

Cont to inc into st st as set on every rs row until there are 58sts. Cont in patt as set without shaping and, when work measures 14cm from the bottom of neck rib, ending with a ws row, place a marker at each end of row to mark top of leg hole.

Next row (rs): k20, [p2, k2] 4 times, p2, k20.

Next row: k1, p19, [k2, p2] 4 times, k2, p19, k1.

These 2 rows form patt.

Cont in patt until work measures 8cm from marker, ending with a ws row. Place second marker at each end of row to mark bottom of leg hole.

Shape rump

Next row (dec row) (rs): k3, k2tog, patt to last 5sts, k2tog, k3. (56sts)

Next row: k1, patt to last st, k1. Work the dec row on next and every 4th row until there are 46sts.

Next row: k14, [p2, k2] 4 times, p2, k14.

Next row: k1, p13, [k2, p2] 4 times, k2, p13, k1. Rep last 2 rows until under panel measures 30cm from bottom of neck rib.

Rib border

Change to 3.5mm needles and set edge rib:

Row 1 (rs): k1, k1tbl, [p2, k2tbl] to last 4sts, p2, k1tbl, k1.

Row 2: k1, p1, [k2, p2] to last 4sts, k2, p1, k1. These 2 rows set rib patt. Cont in patt until rib measures 2cm. Cast off loosely in patt.

TO MAKE UP

Block both panels to the sizes shown in the diagram. Sew up both shoulder seams from the top leg hole marker up to the bottom of the neck rib on one side, and up to the top of neck rib on the other side, turning the seam to the other side halfway up the neck rib, so that the seam does not show when the neck is rolled down.

Leg hole border

With 3.5mm needles and rs facing, pick up 34sts in between the remaining markers for one leg hole.

Next row (ws): [p2, k2] to last 2sts, p2.

Next row: [k2tbl, p2] to last 2sts, k2tbl. These 2 rows set rib patt. Rep these 2 rows 8 times more. Cast off loosely in patt. Work second leg hole border to match. Sew up side seams, noting that the under panel is shorter than the top panel. Weave in all loose ends.

🐾 **FACT FILE**

TINKERBELL
....

Breed: Shiatsu/Poodle cross.
Character: A very happy little dog, always eager to please.
Happiest When: Running and chasing her big sister, Molly the Labrador.
Will Do Anything For: Treats – any kind of treats.
Naughtiest Habit: Digging holes in the garden.
Favourite Treat: Gravy bones.
Hobbies Include: Barking at any dog on the television, dancing and running.

Tinkerbell's Beautiful Basketweave Jumper

If you are new to knitting, this basketweave pattern is a good example of how basic knit and purl stitches can create detailed texture. The moss stitch on the edging, leg bands and collar (which was inspired by yet another of my favourite cardigans) complements the basketweave pattern.

Size
Dog measurements
Neck 23–28cm
Shoulder 10–14cm
Chest 32–38cm
Length 32cm
See Measure Your Dog
   (page 95)

Garment measurements
Neck 22cm unstretched
Chest 33cm unstretched
Length 29cm plus collar

Yarn
4 x 25g balls of Erika Knight
   British Blue in Pretty 042

Needles and equipment
Pair each of 3.5mm and 4mm
   knitting needles
4 safety pins to use as markers
   for leg holes
1 stitch holder
Knitter's sewing needle

Tension
24sts and 30 rows over
   basketweave patt to a 10cm
   square using 4mm needles.

Abbreviations
See page 94.

TOP PANEL
Starting at the lower edge and with 3.5mm needles, cast on 41sts.
Set moss stitch patt
Row 1 (rs): [k1, p1] to last st, k1.
Rep this row 9 times more.
Change to 4mm needles.
Set basketweave patt
Row 1 (rs): knit.
Row 2: k1, p to last st, k1.
Row 3: k1, [p2, k6] to end.
Row 4: knit the knits and purl the purls.
Row 5: knit.
Row 6: k1, p to last st, k1.
Row 7: k5, [p2, k6] to last 4sts, p2, k2.
Row 8: as row 4.
These 8 rows set the basketweave patt and are repeated throughout the panel.
Row 1 (inc row) (rs): k2, M1, k to last 2sts, M1, k2. *(43sts)*
Keeping patt correct, work rows 2–4 of patt.

Row 5 (inc row): k2, M1, k to last 2sts, M1, k2. *(45sts)*
Keeping patt correct, work rows 6–8 of patt.
Cont in patt, inc on rows 1 and 5 as set, until there are 49sts.
Cont in patt without shaping until work measures approximately 18cm from cast on edge, ending with row 4 of patt.

Shape leg
Keeping patt as set:
Row 1 (rs): cast off 4sts, k to end. *(45sts)*
Row 2: cast off 4sts, p to last st, k1. *(41sts)*

Row 3: k5, [p2, k6] to last 4sts, p2, k2.
Row 4: knit the knits and purl the purls.
Row 5: knit.
Row 6: k1, p to last st, k1.
Row 7: k1, [p2, k6] to end.
Row 8: as row 4.

Cont in patt without shaping until leg hole measures 5cm. Place a marker at each end of row to mark top of leg hole. Cont in patt without shaping until work measures 29cm from cast on edge, ending with a ws row. Put these 41sts onto a stitch holder and lightly block this panel; don't flatten it off too much.

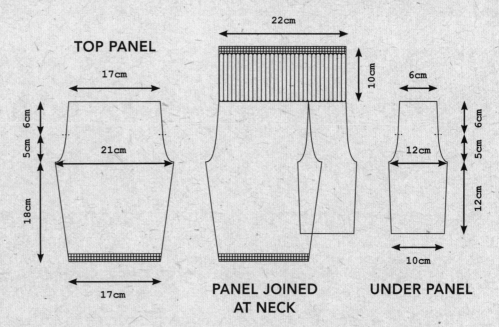

TOP PANEL

17cm
6cm
5cm
21cm
18cm
17cm

22cm
10cm

PANEL JOINED AT NECK

6cm
6cm
12cm
5cm
12cm
10cm

UNDER PANEL

UNDER PANEL
Starting at the lower edge and with 3.5mm needles, cast on 24sts.
Set rib patt
Row 1 (rs): k3, [p2, k2] to last 5sts, p2, k3.
Row 2: k1, p2, [k2, p2] to last 5sts, k2, p2, k1.
These 2 rows set rib patt.
Rep rows 1–2 twice more.
Change to 4mm needles.
Next row (inc row) (rs): k2, M1, k1, [p2, k2] to last 5sts, p2, k1, M1, k2. (26sts)
Next row: k1, p3, [k2, p2] to last 6sts, k2, p3, k1.
Keeping edge sts in st st, cont to inc on every 4th row as set until there are 30sts.
Cont in patt without shaping until work measures 12cm from cast on edge, ending with a ws row.
Shape leg
Next row (rs): cast off 3sts, patt to end. (27sts)
Next row: cast off 3sts, patt to end. (24sts)
Next row (dec row): k2, k2tog, patt to last 4sts, k2tog, k2. (22sts)
Cont to dec as set on every alt rs row until there are 18sts.
Work straight until leg hole measures 5cm, and place a marker at each end of row to mark top of leg hole.

Cont in patt without shaping until work matches top panel from leg hole, ending with a ws row.
Join neck
Change to 3.5mm needles.
Patt 18sts of under panel, then patt 41sts of top panel on stitch holder. (59sts)

COLLAR
Note: row 1 is rs of collar, but ws of body is facing.
Set collar patt
Row 1 (rs): k1, p1, k1, [p3, Tw2] 10 times, p3, k1, p1, k1.

Row 2: k1, p1, k1 [k3, p2] 10 times, k3, k1, p1, k1.
These 2 rows set collar patt.
Cont in patt until collar measures 9cm, ending with a ws row.
Next row (rs): [k1, p1] to last st, k1.
Next row: [k1, p1] to last st, k1.
Rep last 2 rows once more.
Cast off loosely in patt.

TO MAKE UP

Sew up the shoulder seam from top leg marker to lower 5cm of collar; top 5cm of collar stays open.
With rs facing and 3.5mm needles, pick up 23sts along the leg hole, from the leg shaping on the top panel, up to the top leg marker and down to the start of the leg shaping on the under panel. It doesn't matter if you pick up more stitches, but do not pick up fewer, and ensure you have an odd number.
Set moss stitch patt
Next row (ws): [k1, p1] to last st, k1.
Next row: [k1, p1] to last st, k1.
Rep last 2 rows once more.
Cast off loosely in patt.

Work the second leg to match. Sew up the leg seams and then sew the top panel to the under panel, noting that the under panel is shorter than the top panel.
Weave in all loose ends.

🐾 FACT FILE

GLADYS
....

Breed: Italian Greyhound.
Character: Lively, bouncy and cuddly, with a naughty side.
Happiest When: Being chased and not being caught!
Will Do Anything For: Cuddles and kisses.
Naughtiest Habit: Burying her dinner in the sofa and investigating the cat litter tray...
Favourite Treat: Almonds and tea.
Hobbies Include: Snoozing in a comfy bed and munching on a rawhide chew.

Gladys's Roomy Raglan Jumper

I have been hooked on cable stitch ever since I did a workshop on them, which helped me to embrace this wonderful way of knitting texture. The cable on this jumper is a very simple one, ideal for someone new to this lovely technique and the raglan sleeve gives your hound plenty of room to run around in.

Size

Dog measurements
Neck 25–30cm
Neck Length 8cm
Shoulder 12–13cm
Chest 40–50cm
Length 41cm
See Measure Your Dog
  (page 95)

Garment measurements
Neck 22cm unstretched
Chest 36cm unstretched
Length 35cm plus collar

Yarn

2 x 50g balls of Yarn Stories
  Fine Merino & Baby Alpaca DK
  in Cobalt

Needles and equipment

Pair each of 3.5mm and 4mm
  knitting needles
Set of 4 x 3.5mm double-pointed
  needles
Cable needle
2 stitch markers
2 stitch holders
Knitter's sewing needle

Tension

36sts and 30 rows over cable patt
  (unstretched) to a 10cm square
  using 4mm needles.

Abbreviations

See page 94.

CABLE PATT

Row 1 (rs): [k4, p2] 6 times, k4.
Row 2: [p4, k2] to last 4sts, p4.
Row 3 (cable row): [C4F, p2, C4B, p2] to last 4sts, C4F.
Row 4: as row 2.
Row 5: as row 1.
Row 6: as row 2.
Row 7: as row 1.
Row 8: as row 2.
Row 9: (cable row): [C4B, p2, C4F, p2] to last 4sts, C4B.
Row 10: as row 2.
Row 11: as row 1.
Row 12: as row 2.
Row 13: as row 1.
Row 14: as row 2.
Row 15: as row 1.
Row 16: as row 2.

These 16 rows set the cable patt and are repeated on the 40sts of the top panel throughout the length of the jumper.

JUMPER

Starting at the neck edge and with 3.5mm needles, cast on 76sts.

Next row (rs): [k4, p2] to last 4sts, k4.

Next row: [p4, k2] to last 4sts, p4. These 2 rows set rib patt. Cont in patt until rib measures 6cm from cast on edge, ending with a ws row. Cut yarn.

Change to 4mm needles. Divide sts to form under panel and top panel as folls:

Slip 22sts onto a stitch holder (*22sts for under panel*), rejoin yarn to rem sts. (*54sts*)

Row 1 (rs): k4, k2tog twice (*6sts for first leg*), place marker, [k4, p2] 6 times, k4 (*40 sts for top panel, row 1 of cable patt*), place marker, k6 (*6sts for second leg*). (*52sts*)

Row 2: p6, slm, work row 2 of cable patt, slm, p6.

Row 3 (inc row): k1, M1, k4, M1, k1, slm, work row 3 of cable patt, slm, k1, M1, k4, M1, k1. (*56sts*)

Row 4: p8, work row 4 of cable patt, p8.

Row 5 (inc row): k1, M1, k6, M1, k1, slm, work row 5 of cable patt, slm, k1, M1, k6, M1, k1. (*60sts*)

Row 6: p10, slm, work row 6 of cable patt, slm, p10.

Row 7 (inc row): k1, M1, k8, M1, k1, slm, work row 7 of cable patt,
slm, k1, M1, K8, M1, k1. (*64sts*)

Row 8: p12, slm, work row 8 of cable patt, slm, p12.

Row 9 (inc row): k1, M1, k10, M1, k1, slm, work row 9 of cable patt, slm, k1, M1, k10, M1, k1. (*68sts*)

Row 10: p14, slm, work row 10 of cable patt, slm, p14.

Row 11 (inc row): k1, M1, k12, M1, k1, slm, work row 11 of cable patt, slm, k1, M1, k12, M1, k1. (*72sts*)

Row 12: p16, slm, work row 12 of cable patt, slm, p16.

Row 13 (inc row): k1, M1, k14, M1, k1, slm, work row 13 of cable
patt, slm, k1, M1, k14, M1, k1. (*76sts*)

Row 14: p18, slm, work row 14 of cable patt, slm, p18.

Row 15 (inc row): k1, M1, k16, M1, k1, slm, work row 15 of cable patt, slm, k1, M1, k16, M1, k1. (*80sts*)

Row 16: p20, slm, work row 16 of cable patt, slm, p20.

Row 17 (inc row): k1, M1, k18, M1, k1, slm, work row 1 of cable patt, slm, k1, M1, k18, M1, k1. (*84sts*)

Cont to work in cable patt as set from row 2 but without incs

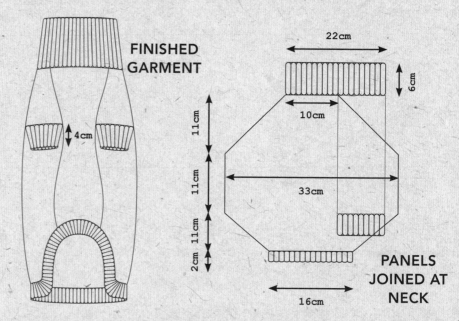

FINISHED GARMENT

11cm

11cm

11cm

2cm

4cm

22cm

6cm

10cm

33cm

16cm

PANELS JOINED AT NECK

until 32 rows of cable patt are completed.

Divide for legs

Next row (row 1 of cable patt) (rs): cut off working yarn, put the first leg sts onto a piece of waste yarn (not a stitch holder as these are bulky and get in the way of your knitting), rejoin working yarn to top panel sts, work row 1 of cable patt across top panel sts, put the second leg sts onto a piece of waste yarn, cast on 22sts.

Next row: p8, k2, p4, k2, p4, k2, work row 2 of cable patt across top panel sts, cast on 22sts.

Next row: k8, p2, k4, p2, k4, p2, work row 3 of cable patt, p2, k4, p2, k4, p2, k8.

UNDER PANEL

Cont in patt as set, and on the next cable row work the new rib sts as the cables, but keep the edge 8sts on each side as st st. Cont in patt as set until work measures 11cm from beginning of leg, ending with a ws row and making a note of which row you are on.

Shape rump

Next row (dec row) (rs): k2, k2tog, patt to last 4sts, k2, k2tog. *(82sts)*

Work one ws row in patt.

Next row (dec row): k2, k2tog, patt to last 4sts, k2tog, k2. *(80sts)*

Cont to knit in patt with decs as set, working k2tog 2sts in from the edge on every rs row until there are 52sts and work measures approximately 33cm from bottom of neck rib.

Put these 52sts onto a stitch holder.

With rs facing and 4mm needles, rejoin yarn to under panel sts.

Row 1 (rs): [k4, p2] 3 times, k4.

Row 2: [p4, k2] 3 times, p4.

Row 3: k4, p2, C4B, p2, C4F, p2, k4.

Row 4: as row 2.

Row 5: as row 1.

Row 6: as row 2.

Row 7: as row 1.

Row 8: as row 2.

Row 9: k4, p2, C4F, p2, C4B, p2, k4.

Row 10: as row 2.

Rows 11–16: rep rows 1–2, 3 times more.

Cont in patt as set until work measures 22cm from bottom of neck rib, matching the start of the rump shaping of top panel, placing a marker at 11cm to mark the leg opening.

Put these 22sts onto a stitch holder.

TO MAKE UP

Lay out the knitting and block the edges gently to the measurements required.

Sew the top panel to the under panel along the left seam from the bottom up, taking care to match the leg opening with the marker on the under panel. Rep for other side.

Rib border

With rs facing and 3.5mm dpns, [k4, p2] 3 times, k4, work across under panel 22sts, pick up 20sts along the left top panel shaped edge, [k4, p2] across the top panel 52sts, pick up 20sts along the right side top panel shaped edge to complete the round. *(114sts)*

Place marker and commence working in the round.

Next round: [k4, p2] to end.

This round sets rib patt. Cont in patt until rib measures 2cm.

Cast off loosely in patt.

Leg hole border

With rs facing and 3.5mm dpns, pick up 22sts along cast off edge of leg hole, then knit the 22sts from the waste yarn. *(44sts)*

Place a marker at beg of round.

Round 1: [k2, p2] to end.

Rep this round until leg measures 4cm.

Cast off loosely in patt.

Work second leg hole border to match.

Weave in all loose ends.

Abbreviations

alt alternate

C2(4)(6)B Cable 2(4)(6) back: slip the next stitch (2 stitches) (3 stitches) onto a cable needle and hold at back of work, knit the next stitch (2 stitches) (3 stitches) on the left-hand needle, then knit the stitch (2 stitches) (3 stitches) from the cable needle.

C2(4)(6)F Cable 2 (4)(6) front: slip the next stitch (2 stitches) (3 stitches) onto a cable needle and hold at front of work, knit the next stitch (2 stitches) (3 stitches) on the left-hand needle, then knit the stitch (2 stitches) (3 stitches) from the cable needle.

cc contrast colour

cont continue(ing)

Cr1b Cross 1 back: slip the next stitch onto a cable needle and hold at back of work, knit the next 2 stitches on the left-hand needle, then purl the stitch from the cable needle.

Cr2f Cross 2 front: slip the next 2 stitches onto a cable needle and hold at front of work, purl the next stitch on the left-hand needle, then knit the 2 stitches from the cable needle.

dec(s) decrease(s)/decreasing

dpn(s) double-pointed needle(s)

foll(s) follow(s)/following

inc(s) increase(s)/increasing

k knit

k1b knit 1 below: insert right needle into next stitch one row below and knit.

k2tog knit 2 stitches together.

lh left hand

M1 make a stitch: from the front pick up the bar between the last stitch worked and the next stitch, place it on the left-hand needle and knit into the back of it.

mc main colour

p purl

p2tog purl 2 stitches together.

patt pattern

rem remain(ing)

rep repeat

rh right hand

rs right side

slm slip marker(s)

st(s) stitch(es)

st st stocking stitch

T.2 knit two stitches together, don't slip them off the left-hand needle, then knit into the first stitch again and slip both original stitches off the left-hand needle.

tbl work through the back of the stitch, not the front.

tog together

Tw2 knit into the second stitch on the left-hand needle and lift it over the first stitch, then knit into the first stitch as normal.

ws wrong side

yo yarn over

Measure Your Dog

Measure your dog before you start knitting a jumper from this book. By altering a few stitches or lengths in key areas, you will be able to obtain a great fit.

The most important measurements are:

A Neck: this will enable you to decide if you need more stitches in the neck rib, as ideally the rib needs to be relaxed when sitting on the dog's neck, and must stretch over the head to put the jumper on.

B Length: measure from your dog's neck along the spine to where you want the jumper to end. Most of the jumpers are designed to be at least 10cm from the top of the tail, but the coats are designed to go all the way to the top of the tail.

C Shoulder: this is important to obtain a good fit. Measure from the centre of your dog's neck – where the collar sits at the top of the spine – diagonally down to the top of the leg, and do the same with your knitting (see diagram). By getting this measurement right, the jumper will not pull back or slouch forward, but will fit comfortably on the dog.

D Chest: use a tape measure to measure all the way around your dog's chest, just behind the front legs. This will tell you if you need to add in some stitches before you get to the leg shaping on the jumpers.

Some of the patterns are knitted from the top down, which means you can try them on your dog as you knit. The coats are easy; just lay the knitting onto your dog to check if it is long enough.

And don't forget that knitting is so forgiving! It stretches and relaxes, so generally the patterns will fit the breeds they are designed for.

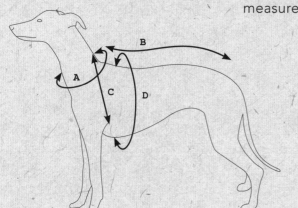

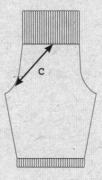

Top Tips

Here are some ideas and advice that I have found useful when knitting the jumpers in this book.

🐾 Always have a notebook to mark off rows and stitch counts.

🐾 Before casting on, mark out the stitches in your notebook in tens and any odd number, then tick off each group as you go. This way, if you get distracted, you will know how many stitches you have cast on.

🐾 When doing a cable stitch, I find it easier to use a cable hook, and I always put the stitches back onto the left-hand needle to knit, rather than knitting them from the cable needle itself.

🐾 I favour a cable cast on, as it gives a good defined edge.

🐾 If your pattern is finished in rib, cast off in pattern for a neater edge; so knit the knit stitches and purl the purl stitches as you cast off across the row.

🐾 Knit with good needles that you feel comfortable with. I like vintage plastic, and use a light coloured pair for dark yarn and a dark coloured pair for light yarn so I can see my stitches easily.

🐾 Learn to 'read' your knitting, so that you can see what you should be doing next, and then you don't have to constantly refer to the pattern. So, for instance, if you are doing a single moss stitch edge, you can 'read' where you did a knit stitch on the row before and need to do a purl on the next row.

🐾 Always do a tension square. This is essential to the fit of your dog's jumper, as you might need to knit on smaller needles if your swatch is coming up big, or on bigger needles if it is coming up small.

🐾 When knitting in the round, keep the right side on the inside of your knitting, so that you are always looking at the right side. This makes it easier to 'read' the knitting as you go.

🐾 When picking up stitches for edges or legs, have the right side facing you, and your first row will be a wrong side row.

🐾 If you would like to substitute a yarn for one that you might have in your stash, there is no reason not to, but you must do a tension square and check it against the tension quoted in the pattern, to be sure that your jumper won't be teeny tiny or too big. No matter how much we all love knitting, having a garment that your dog can't fit into after all your hard work will diminish your pleasure.

🐾 I often knit patterns in different yarns, but be mindful that if I have used a chunky yarn, substitute it with another chunky yarn; similarly if I have used a DK yarn, do the same.

🐾 Measure your dog before you start a project, and adjust the pattern as necessary. For instance, if your dog has a chest 2cm bigger than that of the jumper, and you know that you knit two stitches to 1cm, you will need to adjust the amount of stitches you increase by four, so make two more increases in the chest area. Make a note on the pattern before you start knitting.

About the Author

Based in an Old Barn on the Weald of Kent, Redhound for Dogs produces British-made dog attire and accessories. Inspired by her passion for high-quality, well-fitted clothing and her beloved hounds, Bruno and Frankie, Debbie Humphreys launched the Redhound design brand in 2010. The online shop offers dog jumpers, knitting kits and 'Sew it Yourself' dog coat patterns, alongside bandanas, wax coats, bags and collars. Redhound was awarded Editor's Choice at their first Country Living Show in 2010, and a Runner Up in the prestigious Country Homes & Interiors Rural Business Awards in 2011. Their unique Dog Jumper Knitting Kits have been stocked by many independent shops as well as well-known stores such as Habitat. They collaborated with Holland & Holland on an exclusive range of bespoke dog coats, and have a successful store on the popular market place notonthehighstreet.com.

Acknowledgements

Writing this book has long been a dream of mine, and there are many people I would like to thank for making it a reality.

My yarn suppliers – special thanks go to:
❄ David at Rowan for his support (www.knitrowan.com).
❄ Erika and Arabella at Erika Knight for the yarn and the encouragement (www.erikaknight.co.uk).
❄ Danielle at Yarn Stories for her lovely yarn and cheery emails (www.yarnstories.com).
❄ Carol Ann at Thomas B. Ramsden for her prompt and friendly service (www.tbramsden.co.uk).
❄ And Louisa Harding for creating fantastic yarns (www.louisaharding.co.uk).

My knitters – without you I could not have done it! Huge thanks to:
❄ Marion, for always putting up with my (sometimes erratic) timings!
❄ Brenda, for putting up with fluffy yarn in order to get jumpers knitted on time.

❄ Eve, for being so calm and efficient on every project I gave you.
❄ Lis, for working under pressure to ensure the projects were completed on time.

My dog models – who inspired this book and modelled the jumpers to perfection! And thanks to their owners for bringing them along, and helping us to capture great images. Thank you to Bear, Daisy, Dylan, Edie, Tinkerbell, Ralph, Bunny Mouse, Gladys, Nelly, Pippin, Archie, Scout, Shadow Buster, Alfie, Murray, Frankie and Bruno.

My photographer – huge thanks must go to Kerry Jordan for her amazing photography. Kerry is always accommodating and flexible, and loved by all the dogs. Thank you so much, this is by far the best photo shoot we have done, and I hope there will be many more to come (www.whippetsnippets.co.uk).

Uncle Bill and Auntie Irene – we could not have had such beautiful photographs if it hadn't been for the fantastic location, so for this I wish to thank my wonderful and inspiring Uncle Bill and Auntie Irene for letting us use the grounds of their fantastic home and railway (www.bwlr.co.uk).

My publisher, Pavilion – thank you to Katie Cowan for seeing the potential in me, to my editor Krissy for holding my hand throughout and to my designer, Zoe, for her work on the layouts.

My technical support – for this I thank Kate Haxell and Marilyn Wilson for all their hard work in polishing up my patterns and providing great sketches.

And finally... There are two people who I wish to express extra special thanks to. David my wonderful husband who is always by my side supporting me and who took on just about every domestic duty while I knitted my way through the winter to get the designs and patterns ready. And to Brenda, customer turned mentor turned friend. Thank you for your knitting, support and encouragement, and for helping me see the bigger picture.